✧ *Companions for the Journey* ✧

Praying with
John Baptist de La Salle

✧ *Companions for the Journey* ✧

Praying with
John Baptist de La Salle

by
Carl Koch, FSC

Saint Mary's Press
Christian Brothers Publications
Winona, Minnesota

✧   *To my Brothers*   ✧

The publishing team for this book included Cheryl Drivdahl, copy editor; Holly Storkel, production editor and typesetter; and Elaine Kohner, illustrator; pre-press, printing, and binding by the graphics division of Saint Mary's Press.

The acknowledgments continue on page 109.

Printed in the United States of America

Printing: 6 5 4 3 2 1

Year: 1995 94 93 92 91 90

ISBN 0-88489-240-9

✧ Contents ✧

✧ Foreword ✧

Companions for the Journey

Just as food is required for human life, so are companions. Indeed, the word *companions* comes from two Latin words: *com*, meaning "with," and *panis*, meaning "bread." Companions nourish our heart, mind, soul, and body. They are also the people with whom we can celebrate the sharing of bread.

Perhaps the most touching stories in the Bible are about companionship: the Last Supper, the wedding feast at Cana, the sharing of the loaves and the fishes, and Jesus' breaking of bread with the disciples on the road to Emmaus. Each incident of companionship with Jesus revealed more about his mercy, love, wisdom, suffering, and hope. When Jesus went to pray in the Garden of Olives, he craved the companionship of the Apostles. They let him down. But God sent the Spirit to inflame the hearts of the Apostles, and they became faithful companions to Jesus and to each other.

Throughout history, other faithful companions have followed Jesus and the Apostles. These saints and mystics have also taken the journey from conversion, through suffering, to resurrection. Just as they were inspired by the holy people who went before them, so too may you take them as your companions as you walk on your spiritual journey.

The Companions for the Journey series is a response to the spiritual hunger of Christians. This series makes available the rich spiritual teachings of mystics and guides whose wisdom can help us on our pilgrimages. As you complete the last meditation in each volume, it is hoped that you will feel supported, challenged, and affirmed by a soul-companion on your spiritual journey.

The spiritual hunger that has emerged over the last twenty years is a great sign of renewal in Christian life. People fill retreat programs and workshops on topics in spirituality. The demand for spiritual directors exceeds the number available. Interest in the lives and writings of saints and mystics is increasing as people search for models of whole and holy Christian life.

Praying with De La Salle

Praying with John Baptist de La Salle is more than just a book about De La Salle's spirituality. This book seeks to engage you in praying in the way that De La Salle did about issues and themes that were central to his experience. Each meditation can enlighten your understanding of his spirituality and lead you to reflect on your own experience.

The goal of *Praying with John Baptist de La Salle* is that you will discover De La Salle's profound spirituality and integrate his spirit and wisdom into your relationship with God, with your brothers and sisters, and with your own heart and mind.

Suggestions for Praying with De La Salle

Meet John Baptist de La Salle, a courageous and fascinating companion for your pilgrimage, by reading the introduction to this book, which begins on page 13. It provides a brief biography of De La Salle and an outline of the major themes of his spirituality.

Once you meet De La Salle, you will be ready to pray with him and to encounter God, your sisters and brothers, and yourself in new and wonderful ways. To help your prayer, here are some suggestions that have been part of the tradition of Christian spirituality:

Create a sacred space. Jesus said, "When you pray, go to your private room, shut yourself in, and so pray to your [God] who is in that secret place, and your [God] who sees all that is done in secret will reward you" (Matthew 6:6). Solitary prayer is best done in a place where you can have privacy and silence, both of which can be luxuries in the lives of busy people. If privacy and silence are not possible, create a quiet, safe place within yourself, perhaps while riding to and from work, while sitting in line at the dentist's office, or while waiting for someone. Do the best you can, knowing that a loving God is present everywhere. Whether the meditations in this book are used for solitary prayer or with a group, try to create a prayerful mood with candles, meditative music, an open Bible, or a crucifix.

Open yourself to the power of prayer. Every human experience has a religious dimension. All of life is suffused with God's presence. So remind yourself that God is present as you begin your period of prayer. Do not worry about distractions. If something keeps intruding during your prayer, spend some time talking with God about it. Be flexible because God's Spirit blows where it will.

Prayer can open your mind and widen your vision. Be open to new ways of seeing God, people, and yourself. As you open yourself to the Spirit of God, different emotions are evoked, such as sadness from tender memories, or joy from a celebration recalled. Our emotions are messages from God that can tell us much about our spiritual quest. Also, prayer strengthens our will to act. Through prayer, God can touch our will and empower us to live according to what we know is true.

Finally, many of the meditations in this book will call you to employ your memories, your imagination, and the circumstances of your life as subjects for prayer. The great mystics and saints realized that they had to use all their resources to know God better. Indeed, God speaks to us continually and touches us constantly. We must learn to listen and feel with all the means that God gave us.

Come to prayer with an open mind, heart, and will.

Preview each meditation before beginning. Spend a few moments previewing the readings and especially the reflection activities. Several reflection activities are given in each meditation because different styles of prayer appeal to different personalities or personal needs. **Note that each meditation has more reflection activities than can be done during one prayer period. Therefore, select only one or two reflection activities each time you use a meditation. Do not feel compelled to complete all of the reflection activities.**

Read meditatively. After you have placed yourself in God's presence, the meditations offer you a story about De La Salle and a reading from his writings. Take your time reading. If a particular phrase touches you, stay with it. Relish its feelings, meanings, and concerns.

Use the reflections. Following the readings is a short reflection in commentary form meant to give perspective to the readings. Then you will be offered several ways of meditating on the readings and the theme of the prayer. You may be familiar with the different methods of meditating, but in case you are not, they are described briefly here:

✦ *Repeated short prayer or mantra:* One means of focusing your prayer is to use a *mantra*, or prayer word. The mantra may be a single word or a short phrase taken from the readings or from the Scriptures. For example, a mantra for a meditation on faith might be "I go before you" or "trust." Repeated slowly in harmony with your breathing, the mantra helps you center your heart and mind on one action or attribute of God.

✦ *Lectio divina:* This type of meditation is "divine studying," a concentrated reflection on the word of God or the wisdom of a spiritual writer. Most often in *lectio divina*, you will be invited to read one of the passages several times and then concentrate on one or two sentences, pondering their meaning for you and their effect on you. *Lectio divina* commonly ends with formulation of a resolution.

✦ *Guided meditation:* In this type of meditation, our imagination helps us consider alternative actions and likely consequences. Our imagination helps us experience new ways of seeing God, our neighbors, ourselves, and nature. When Jesus told his followers parables and stories, he engaged their imagination. In this book, you will be invited to follow guided meditations.

One way of doing a guided meditation is to read the scene or story several times until you know the outline and can recall it when you enter into reflection. Or before your prayer time, you may wish to record the meditation on a tape recorder. If so, remember to allow pauses for reflection between phrases and to speak with a slow, peaceful pace and tone. Then during prayer, when you have finished the readings and the reflection commentary, you can turn on your recording of the meditation and be led through it. If you find your own voice too distracting, ask a friend to make the tape for you.

✦ *Examen of consciousness:* The reflections often will ask you to examine how God has been speaking to you in your past and present experience—in other words, the reflections will ask you to examine your awareness of God's presence in your life.

✦ *Journal writing:* Writing is a process of discovery. If you write for any length of time, stating honestly what is on your mind and in your heart, you will unearth much about who you are, how you stand with your God, what deep longings reside in your soul, and more. In some reflections, you will be asked to write a dialog with Jesus or someone else. If you have never used writing as a means of meditation, try it. Reserve a special notebook for your journal writing. If desired, you can go back to your entries at a future time for an examen of consciousness.

✦ *Action:* Occasionally, a reflection will suggest singing a favorite hymn, going out for a walk, or undertaking some other physical activity. Actions can be meaningful forms of prayer.

Using the Meditations for Group Prayer

If you wish to use the meditations for community prayer, these suggestions may help:

✦ Read the theme to the group. Call the community into the presence of God, using the short opening prayer. Invite one or two participants to read one or both of the readings. If you use both readings, observe the pause between them.

✦ The reflection commentary may be used as a reading, or it can be deleted, depending on the needs and interests of the group.

✦ Select one of the reflection activities for your group. Allow sufficient time for your group to reflect, to do a centering prayer or mantra, to accomplish a studying prayer (*lectio divina*), or to finish an examen of consciousness. Depending on the group and the amount of available time, you may want to invite the participants to share their reflections, responses, or petitions with the group.

✦ Reading the passage from the Scriptures may serve as a summary of the meditation.

✦ If a formulated prayer or a psalm is given as a closing, it may be recited by the entire group. Or you may ask participants to offer their own prayers for the closing.

Now you are ready to begin praying with John Baptist de La Salle, a faithful and caring companion on this stage of your spiritual journey. De La Salle has inspired many people to seek a closer relationship with God. It is hoped that you will find him to be a true soul-companion.

✧ Introduction ✧

De La Salle: Led by the Spirit

John Baptist de La Salle never inspired the popular devotion that people show toward Francis of Assisi, Thérèse de Lisieux, or Anthony of Padua. His name may be recognized only by people who attended a school staffed by the Brothers of the Christian Schools.

True, De La Salle founded a major religious congregation. He was proclaimed the patron of teachers by Pope Pius XII. He systematized and made practical many of the educational methods considered standard practice today, such as teaching an entire group of pupils simultaneously and giving regular, individual reports about students' progress. He started a teacher training center, uncommon in his time. But few Christians know anything about him.

Why should twentieth-century Christians be interested in or inspired by De La Salle's spirituality? Like most of us, De La Salle experienced no blinding visions or voices out of the thunder telling him what God wanted him to do. Instead, like us, he listened to people, saw needs, felt compassion, and prayed for God's spirit.

French society disdained teaching in charity schools as a work fit only for those who could do nothing better. Despite strenuous objections from his relatives and friends, De La Salle, who was a member of a distinguished family, not only formed a community of teachers to serve poor people but gave away his wealth and position to live like them.

In short, De La Salle held firmly to his beliefs. Holding fast to his course in life often demanded heroic faith and courage. At the same time, De La Salle showed that following the way of the Gospels in ordinary tasks, no matter how humble, can lead to holiness and the touch of God's love. For De La Salle, spirituality and day-to-day decisions about practical matters could not be separated. When he told his Brothers how to teach writing to the children, he was telling them how to love the children. When done in the spirit of faith—that is, seeing each child as sacred to God—every act of service becomes a prayer. Thus, De La Salle's spirituality is for the workplace and the home, the classroom and the streets.

De La Salle's Early Years

John Baptist de La Salle was born in 1651, early in the reign of the Sun King, Louis XIV, and in the middle of *Le Grand Siecle*, the century many consider a high point of French culture. He was the eldest of eleven children, of whom seven survived.

Born into a wealthy family of Reims, De La Salle might have eventually moved among the rich and famous of France. Like most children of well-to-do parents, he received tutoring at home until he reached nine years of age. From then until he was eighteen, he studied at the Collège des Bon-Enfants. The school's classical curriculum included grammar and syntax, Latin, Greek, and philosophy.

At age eleven, De La Salle took the first steps toward priesthood by receiving the tonsure, which meant that a patch of hair at the top of his head was shaved. At fifteen, he inherited a canonry at the cathedral of Reims. Becoming a cathedral canon was an honor and provided additional income to De La Salle's family. The canons prayed the Divine Office together daily in the cathedral, participated in the major liturgical feasts, and advised the archbishop. In 1670, De La Salle entered the major seminary of Saint Sulpice in Paris. Here he learned a method of meditative prayer that he would later adapt for his Brothers. As part of the seminary routine on Sundays, he taught religion to children in the parish, which served the most crime-ridden section of Paris.

The course of De La Salle's life changed in 1671 when both of his parents died. Suddenly De La Salle had charge of the family estate and his younger brothers and sisters.

Beginning His Mission

Realizing that he needed a spiritual guide, De La Salle chose Nicolas Roland, a fellow canon at Reims. Unknown to both men, this relationship would lead De La Salle to assume his life's mission.

Roland encouraged De La Salle to finish his studies for the priesthood. At the age of twenty-seven, De La Salle was ordained. Two weeks later, Roland died, having named De La Salle as the executor of his will and protector of the Sisters of the Holy Child Jesus, who were formed to educate poor girls. De La Salle helped the Sisters obtain *letters patent,* or legal status, and continued to say Mass for them and see to their spiritual needs.

One day, as De La Salle was coming to visit the Sisters, he met Adrien Nyel. Nyel was a layman who had come to Reims to establish a charity school for boys at the behest of Mme Jeanne Dubois Maillefer, who was connected by marriage to the De La Salle family. During the chance meeting, Nyel explained his intentions to De La Salle. Offering to help Nyel make the necessary contacts, De La Salle suggested that Nyel stay at his house.

One pastor agreed to establish a charity school for boys in his parish; thus, in April 1679, the first school opened its doors. Soon another donor wished to open a school on the other side of Reims; Nyel obliged. The quarters provided by the parish for Nyel and the other teachers became inadequate. Out of his own pocket, De La Salle rented a house near his own for the teachers. Shortly, Nyel opened a third school in Reims.

Despite the success of the schools, problems arose. The supervision of the schools demanded more attention than Nyel could give. The teachers were young, untrained, and in need of clear direction. The classrooms bulged with boys.

Sizing up the situation, De La Salle decided to invite the teachers into his home for their meals. In this way, he could work with them and, he hoped, improve their skills and motivation as teachers.

His plan worked. The teachers improved and so did order in the schools. Even so, De La Salle was in a quandary. On one hand, he wanted the charity schools to fulfill their mission, but their success would depend on the steady growth of competence among the teachers, a growth largely dependent on his involvement with them. On the other hand, he was not certain how involved he should become with the charity schools and the teachers.

De La Salle sought the advice of Father Nicolas Barré, who had worked to set up schools for poor children in Rouen and Paris. Barré's advice distressed De La Salle. In effect, he suggested that De La Salle live with the schoolmasters.

One contemporary of De La Salle's described those who taught school as "gamblers, drunkards, libertines, ignorant, and brutal." Later in his life, De La Salle admitted, "Those whom I was at first obliged to employ as teachers, I ranked below my own valet, hence the very thought of having to live with them was unbearable" (W. J. Battersby, *St. John Baptist de La Salle*, pp. 41, 71). Nevertheless, De La Salle decided to move the schoolmasters into his own home.

Anger, disbelief, and accusations of madness greeted De La Salle's actions. Relatives removed his younger brothers from his care. De La Salle persevered, believing that providing disciplined, competent teachers was a task given to him by God.

Under De La Salle's tutelage, the teachers increased in competence. Requests came to open other charity schools for boys. Nevertheless, the masters began to grumble about the insecurity and the hard life of religious discipline. De La Salle urged them to rely on Providence, but they reminded him that he did not have to worry if the schools failed because he was independently wealthy.

Once again, De La Salle prayed over the matter and turned to Father Barré for advice. Barré suggested that if De La Salle wanted the charity schools to prosper, he should renounce his canonry and distribute his money to poor people. If God wanted the charity schools established, God would see to it. This radical recommendation was countered by many other voices, but after a long period of prayer, De La Salle resigned his canonry and gave away his wealth to the victims of a famine raging through France. He became as poor and reliant on God's providence as the schoolmasters.

Forming the Community

De La Salle implemented the most useful methods of instruction in the schools and negotiated to open new charity schools. He also began forming the teachers into a religious community. They followed a schedule that included specific times for prayer, meals, and work. Not all of the men were willing to commit themselves to such a lifestyle; some left, a small group stayed.

De La Salle was now totally committed to the community of teachers. To establish their unique identity as laymen dedicated to charity schools, they decided to wear a simple black robe, thick-soled shoes like those worn by peasants, a tricornered hat, and a short mantle or cape. This drab habit distinguished them from clerics and indicated the beginning of a new type of community. It was also practical and fitting for men working with poor children. For instance, the Brothers' mantle was short because, as De La Salle said, "It has been noticed that with [a long mantle] there is a danger of knocking over most of the small children on either side while trying to place them in order" (W. J. Battersby, ed., *De La Salle: Letters and Documents*, p. 257).

Much of De La Salle's zeal for the Christian education of poor children came from his conviction that with an education, people could establish a lifestyle free from hunger and poverty. Poor people in France were oppressed, the victims of a monarchal system that kept every citizen in his or her place on the social ladder. The cheap labor of the peasants and workers supported the extravagant way of life of the aristocracy. In providing a Christian education to poor children, De La Salle helped them both learn their religion and improve their lot in life.

Gradually, somewhat better educated men started asking to be trained as Brothers. De La Salle established a formation program for them. He also created a teacher training school for men who would run schools in rural areas. Even so, the community had no legal standing in France or status within the church.

In 1686, De La Salle persuaded an assembly of Brothers to choose one of their own to be the superior. Reluctantly, they did so. Concerned that a priest should have a Brother as his superior, the archbishop demanded that De La Salle resume direction of the community. This incident points to two important characteristics of De La Salle: his detachment from power and his desire to develop leadership among the Brothers to ensure continuity of direction in the community.

Establishing Schools in Paris

De La Salle then accepted an invitation from the pastor of Saint Sulpice in Paris to take over the charity school there. He knew that if the work he had started was to gain a firm foothold, the Brothers had to become established in France's capital city. So, in 1688, De La Salle set out with two Brothers for Paris.

The school on rue Princesse contained two hundred students from the surrounding slums. In a short time, the Brothers had grouped the boys by age and imposed order and a daily schedule. As was often the case, the priest who had been running the school became jealous of De La Salle's progress and started a rumor campaign against him. Nevertheless, the school thrived, and the Brothers assumed direction of other schools in the parish.

Practical man that he was, De La Salle studied the most effective ways to educate poor children. Eventually, the collected wisdom from these early years in the schools was published in a manual of instructions for teachers titled *The Conduct of the Schools*. This book gave specific guidelines on such topics as "What Is Done During Breakfast and Lunch," "Method of Reading the Chart of Syllables," "Method of Training to Write Well," and "Daily Prayers That Are Said in School." Permeating the methods described are ways of integrating the teaching of the Gospels into all aspects of school life.

Another testimony to De La Salle's practicality and concern for the children's needs was his insistence that French be
the language of instruction. Today, it seems obvious that children learn best in their native tongue, but in De La Salle's
time, elementary schools taught children to read and write
Latin first and gave minimal instruction in French. De La
Salle's reactions to the traditional method may be summarized
this way: Poor children will remain in school for only a short
time. They can learn to read and write more rapidly in their
native language. If they must wait to be instructed in religion
until they know Latin, they will never be proficient enough to

learn about their faith. Therefore, all instruction should begin with French. Some people opposed De La Salle on this matter, but he refused to change, knowing what his children needed.

Problems continued to plague De La Salle. In 1690, the diocesan supervisor of the Little Schools (those charging fees) accused the Brothers of accepting students capable of paying for their education. Over the next years, De La Salle incurred the wrath of the Little Schools masters and the Writing Masters (a guild of professional scribes). The masters of the Little Schools were losing paying students to the Brothers' schools, where there was better discipline and the boys learned more. The Writing Masters wanted to preserve their monopoly on the teaching of penmanship. These two groups filed suits against De La Salle, twice seized the furniture of the schools, forced the closure of the schools for a period, and harassed the small community.

The pastor of Saint Sulpice disliked the habit of the Brothers and pressured De La Salle to change it. De La Salle's refusal caused tension between the two men. Then the pastor attempted to interfere with the formation of the young men who wished to join the community. In fending off this intrusion, De La Salle was labeled "stubborn," a term often used by those who challenged his resolve to maintain the unique identity of the community.

The Brothers led hard lives. Many died young from diseases easily contracted in the crowded schools and decaying slums. Exhaustion and stress from the demands of the ministry made them vulnerable to discouragement. Some left the community to make a better living for themselves, using the skills they had learned as Brothers. De La Salle himself suffered through a near-fatal illness. Then a Brother to whom De La Salle looked for future leadership in the community died suddenly, deeply shocking De La Salle.

By 1691, De La Salle could see that the community stood on the verge of collapse. His solution was to purchase a house just outside Paris. The Brothers came there for rest and retreat, and De La Salle started a novitiate so that young men could be trained in the Brothers' lifestyle with a minimum of interference. De La Salle and two senior Brothers took a vow to build the community even if they were the last ones left and had to live on bread alone. However, more men joined the community, and the crisis was averted.

Spreading the Ministry

De La Salle realized that many poor young men had been working since childhood and lacked any sort of education, especially religious education. So he opened a special program for them. On Sundays and holidays, young workers learned reading, writing, arithmetic, drafting, and religion.

Between 1691 and 1698, De La Salle wrote several important works. In 1694, he developed a rule for the community that would reflect the lived experience of the Brothers. This rule was submitted to the Brothers for their consideration and approval. In addition, De La Salle wrote textbooks that would go through dozens of editions and would be used long after his death: *Rules of Christian Politeness*, which specifies proper manners, conduct, and hygiene for boys; *The Duties of a Christian*, an exposition of Christian teachings; and a little book of prayers for use by the children. De La Salle composed each text to meet the needs of the Brothers and their students.

De La Salle sent Brothers to take over schools in Chartres, Calais, Troyes, Avignon, Rouen, and several other towns. In Rouen, De La Salle opened a boarding school in which "commercial" courses were offered. An innovation because they broke from the classical curriculum, these courses trained students to enter the world of business. When people asked him to take delinquent young men into his care, De La Salle set up the first reformatory in France.

In 1709, another famine swept France, leaving thousands dead. Always living on the edge of destitution, the Brothers suffered along with everyone else. In Chartres alone, five Brothers died. De La Salle and the Brothers persevered, only to face trouble from other sources.

In Paris, a wealthy young man who promised to fund a teacher training center reneged on his agreement and accused

De La Salle of owing him a substantial sum. Using their influence, the young man's family had De La Salle fined and nearly jailed.

In Marseilles, one faction of clerics preferred to have seminarians teach in the charity schools. Also in Marseilles, a significant number of people withdrew their support when they discovered that the Brothers trained in the novitiate could be sent to other parts of France. Even some of the Brothers attacked De La Salle because he called them to task for deviating from the rule of the community.

In his typical response to these conflicts, De La Salle went to a shrine and then to a monastery for retreat, waiting for God's will to become clear. This time has been described as De La Salle's "dark night of the soul." No one is sure exactly what happened during his retreat, but he eventually continued his journey.

At Mende, two Brothers took advantage of De La Salle's embattled position in Paris and the conflict with the Brothers in Marseilles, and refused to let De La Salle stay in the community residence. They knew that De La Salle would challenge their laxity in performing their teaching duties and observing the lifestyle of the community, and, likely, would transfer them to another community. De La Salle found shelter first with the Capuchins and then with a prominent woman who sought his help in writing a rule for a community of women. These incidents only made De La Salle more unsure of his path.

Finally, Brother Timothy, director of the by-then-closed novitiate in Marseilles, found De La Salle at Mende and persuaded him that the Brothers needed and wanted him as their leader. With some reluctance, De La Salle journeyed to Grenoble, where he remained with the Brothers for almost a year.

At Grenoble, De La Salle's chronic rheumatism flared up, crippling him. The cure inflicted as much pain as the illness, but he gradually mended. He revised his writings, substituted in classes, and sought the spiritual direction of Sister Louise, a simple hermit known for her powers of discernment. At age sixty-three, he wondered if the community he had founded was going to survive, or indeed if they wanted or needed him.

Then, in April 1714, De La Salle received a letter from the beleaguered and leaderless Brothers of Paris, ordering him under his vows to return and resume direction of the community. The parish priest of Saint Sulpice who had long sought control of the Brothers' work had set about making changes in their rule. Ecclesiastical superiors were being appointed to direct each community. Sister Louise counseled De La Salle that the letter was a sure sign God wanted him to continue to lead the community. With some delays, De La Salle journeyed back to Paris.

De La Salle's Final Years

De La Salle set matters straight in Paris, then returned to Rouen to guide the novices and work with the delinquents. He also called a general assembly of the Brothers so they could elect a head of the society. In 1717, delegates representing the 103 Brothers gathered and chose Brother Barthélemy as superior.

For the last two years of his life, De La Salle withdrew from any direction of the Brothers, preferring rather to encourage their initiative and decisions. He spent long hours in prayer, and people frequently sought his spiritual guidance. The community grew and spread.

After a long illness, John Baptist de La Salle died on Good Friday, 1719. His last words were spoken in response to a question from Brother Barthélemy: "I adore in all things the holy will of God in my regard" (Battersby, *De La Salle*, p. 290).

De La Salle's Spirituality

De La Salle's spirituality evolved from his experience, and he articulated it gradually. His meditations, letters, memorandums, and books on teaching addressed the problems of the Brothers' day-to-day life and ministry—teaching poor children. He wanted the Brothers to see God working in all aspects of their life. Even though he directed his writings to the Brothers, what he said is relevant for anyone on the spiritual journey.

The Spirit of Faith

Central to Lasallian spirituality is the spirit of faith. De La Salle constantly urged his Brothers to look on all things with the eyes of faith. Essentially, this meant seeing the world as God would. So, for example, if a Brother encountered a stubborn, mischievous boy, he should remind himself that Jesus met resistance even from his disciples and yet patiently taught them. Through prayer and meditation on the Scriptures, faith would grow in the Brothers, and they would encounter and be guided by the Holy Spirit living within them.

De La Salle was convinced that without the spirit of faith, the Brothers would become discouraged and selfish and would eventually abandon the mission to which they were called.

Zeal

De La Salle did not shy away from the word *zeal*. He knew that genuine faith always overflows with generous good works and courageous love. If people rely on God's providence, discern God's will, and acknowledge God's love for them, zeal will energize whatever they do. Believers in Jesus should be known immediately by their zealous love of God and other people.

Nurturing Faith

Having established the spirit of faith and zeal as the foundations of his spirituality, De La Salle constructed the Brothers' lifestyle to nurture and deepen their faith, which overflowed in zeal. He instructed the Brothers to do the following:

✦ *Read the rule of the Gospels.* De La Salle told his Brothers to read the Scriptures every day. In fact, they carried copies of the Christian Scriptures with them wherever they went. Clearly, if the Brothers were to be animated by a faith grounded in Jesus, they had to encounter Jesus in the Scriptures.

✦ *Live in God's presence.* Another way of nurturing faith was to constantly acknowledge the presence of God. De La Salle thought that if the Brothers regularly reminded themselves that God is present they would more likely act as God would want them to. Thus, whenever a Brother entered a room, he knelt down and recalled the presence of God. Every half hour in class, a boy rang a small bell and the prayer leader said, "Let us remember that we are in the holy presence of God."

✦ *Pray always.* Besides meditating on the Scriptures and recalling the presence of God, De La Salle knew that praying regularly and actively was indispensable to nourishing faith. He wrote a method of prayer and meditations for retreats, major feasts, and Sundays.

Trusting in Providence and God's Will

A recurring motif in Lasallian spirituality is complete abandonment to Providence. De La Salle trusted totally in the love God has for everyone. No matter how many times his enemies attacked him, people abandoned him, or poverty left the cupboards bare, De La Salle knew that God would provide.

Closely related to De La Salle's reliance on divine providence was his desire always to do God's will. All through his life, De La Salle turned to spiritual directors, friends, prayer, and study of the Scriptures to discern what God wanted of him.

Ministering to Poor People

De La Salle heard the cries of the poor people in Reims, in Paris, and throughout France. He recognized that poverty, ignorance, and oppression spawned crime, sin, and destruction. Breaking the cycle of poverty into which poor children had been born demanded that those children be given an education with which they could earn a decent living and learn how to live with dignity as Christians. Providing a quality education for children of poor people was a revolutionary act, which De La Salle discerned as his mission from God.

Even though he wanted his Brothers to be highly competent teachers, De La Salle knew that their personal example was essential in the teaching of religion. If the teachers wanted their students to hear and believe the Good News, they must give good example in their own way of living.

De La Salle also saw that each child was different. He devised ways in which the Brothers, like all effective ministers, could touch the heart and mind of each individual child uniquely, kindly, and carefully.

De La Salle for Today

Lasallian spirituality is especially suited for people who get up early, are busy with their job, are concerned about their family, and are trying, in short, to lead Christian lives day by day, within the context of the ordinary. De La Salle taught crowded classes, traveled on foot to administer the schools, coped with legal problems and unjust attacks, suffered from chronic rheumatism, lived in poverty, and yet believed that God would guide and bless him each step of the way.

To travel on our spiritual journey with De La Salle as our companion is to trust, like him, that God will provide for us and lead us on our way.

✧ Meditation 1   ✧

The Spirit of Faith

Theme: Central to Lasallian spirituality is the spirit of faith. De La Salle realized that unless people are animated and guided by a firm belief in the Good News of Jesus Christ, they will wander away from goodness, wisdom, and charity.

Opening prayer: Merciful God, grant me an increase in faith so that I may have hope and love in abundance.

About De La Salle

Many of the difficulties that beset De La Salle were outlined in the introduction to this book. Recall that the Little Schools and the Writing Masters sued him and forced the closure of the schools for a period. Several clerics tried to destroy his reputation and to undermine his leadership. Poverty, hard work, and illness sapped his energies. However,

> throughout all of these difficulties De La Salle retained his characteristic calm, remained in the background as much as possible, and went about his business as usual. With his equally characteristic tenacity, he never surrendered any of the principles that he considered essential to the Brothers and the Christian Schools. . . .
> The secret of De La Salle's imperturbable confidence and calm in the face of opposition and defeat lay in his

deep religious faith, the "spirit of faith," as he called it, that he left as a legacy to his Institute. (Luke Salm, *The Work Is Yours*, p. 125)

An example of what the spirit of faith meant to De La Salle can be seen in a resolution he made for himself while on retreat:

I shall always consider the establishment and the direction of our community as the work of God. That is why I have entrusted it to his care, in such a way that as far as I am concerned, I shall do nothing that concerns the Institute except by his orders. For that reason I shall always consult extensively concerning what I ought to do. I will often speak to God in the words of the prophet Habacuc: *Domine opus tuum*. [Lord, the work is yours.] (Salm, *The Work Is Yours*, p. 126)

Pause: Reflect on how the spirit of faith lives in you, especially in times of difficulty.

De La Salle's Words

Faith should be the light and guide of every Christian, to lead and direct him in the way of salvation. . . .
    The spirit of our Institute is therefore first, a spirit of faith. . . .
    . . . The Brothers of the Society shall animate all their actions with sentiments of faith; and they shall always have in view the orders and the will of God, which they shall adore in all things, and by which they shall be careful to regulate their conduct. (*A Collection of Various Short Treatises*, pp. 57–59)

The spirit of faith is a sharing in the Spirit of God who dwells in us, which leads us to regulate our conduct in all things by the sentiments and truths that faith teaches us. You should, therefore, be wholly occupied in acquiring it, so that it may be for you a shield against the fiery darts of the devil. (*The Letters of John Baptist de La Salle*, p. 217)

Reflection

Love stands as the central norm for Christian living, but De La Salle recognized that love cannot be nurtured without faith. A Brother in a room crowded with poor boys would not last long if he did not believe that he was serving God and that his efforts would ultimately bear fruit. Faith lets us believe in the unseen God and the unseen benefits of our labor.

De La Salle also realized that faith not only motivates us to do good but also instructs us in how to act. Faith could draw a Brother to teach each day, but the Brother must teach as Jesus did or in the manner that faith in Jesus would indicate. Seeing all things through the eyes of faith required the study of the Scriptures and constant prayer.

✧ Forgetting the role that faith plays in our day-to-day activities or in our relationships is easy. To reappropriate your acts of faith, sit quietly. Remind yourself that God is with you. Meditate on each of these questions and record your responses, perhaps in your journal or on a separate sheet of paper:

✦ What actions have I taken today that depend on my faith in the unseen good that will come from those actions?
✦ What relationships of mine are sustained by my faith in the other person?
✦ Who believes in me?

✧ Select one line from "About De La Salle" or "De La Salle's Words" and pray it slowly and repeatedly. Let the meaning and the feelings of the line sink in.

✧ Look ahead to tomorrow's work and to the interactions you will have with other people. List five activities you will do and five people with whom you will be involved. Next to each activity and name, describe how you should act if you are motivated by the spirit of faith.

✧ Pray a litany for an increase in faith, naming specific ways in which you want to grow; for example, "When I become skeptical about the goodness of people, give me faith," or "When I have doubts about Jesus' message of love, give me faith," or "When I become discouraged in the face of difficulties, give me faith."

God's Word

Only faith can guarantee the blessings that we hope for, or prove the existence of realities that are unseen. It is for their faith that our ancestors are acknowledged.

It is by faith that we understand that the ages were created by a word from God, so that from the invisible the visible world came to be. . . .

It was by faith that Abraham obeyed the call to set out for a country that was the inheritance given to him and his descendants. . . .

It was equally by faith that Sarah, in spite of being past the age, was made able to conceive. . . .

It was through faith that the walls of Jericho fell down when the people had marched round them for seven days. It was by faith that Rahab the prostitute welcomed the spies [of Israel] and so was not killed with the unbelievers. . . .

. . . Let us keep our eyes fixed on Jesus, who leads us in our faith and brings it to perfection: for the sake of the joy which lay ahead of him, he endured the cross, disregarding the shame of it, and has taken his seat at the right of God's throne. Think of the way he persevered against such opposition from sinners and then you will not lose heart and come to grief. (Hebrews 11:1—12:3)

Closing prayer: "My God, I offer you all my thoughts, words, and actions of this day, that they may be wholly consecrated to you and that they may procure for me your holy love, which is all I desire. I offer you the new life, which you have given me by waking me from sleep. Let it, I ask you, be to me a life of grace so that I may henceforth be able to say that it is no longer I who live, but that it is Jesus Christ who lives in me." (Adapted from John Baptist de La Salle, *Manual of Piety*, p. 4)

✧   **Meditation 2**   ✧

The Rule of the Scriptures

Theme: The word of God nourishes the spirit of faith. In the sacred Scriptures, we encounter Jesus, who is truth and love.

Opening prayer: Spirit of God, fill me with love for your blessed word.

About De La Salle

"The Spirit of this Institute," [De La Salle wrote,] "is first a Spirit of Faith, which should induce those who compose it not to look upon anything but with the eyes of faith, not to do anything but in view of God, and to attribute all to God, always entering into these sentiments of Job: *The Lord gave and the Lord hath taken away; as it hath pleased the Lord, so is it done,* and into other similar sentiments so often expressed in Holy Scripture and uttered by the Patriarchs of old." Certain practices are then indicated to enable the Brothers "to enter into this Spirit and live accordingly." In the first place they should have "a most profound respect for the Holy Scriptures; and, in proof thereof, always carry the New Testament about them, and pass no day without reading some of it, through a sentiment of faith, respect and veneration for the divine words contained therein, looking upon it as their first and principal rule." (W. J. Battersby, *De La Salle: Saint and Spiritual Writer*, p. 117)

Pause: Consider what impact the Scriptures have in your life.

De La Salle's Words

Jesus Christ, speaking to his apostles, said that he gave an example to them that they might do as he had done. He also wanted his disciples to be with him at all the conversions he brought about, so that they could see how he acted and take him as the rule and model for all they would do to win others to God.

This is also what you must do, since Jesus Christ has chosen you among so many others to be his cooperators in the salvation of souls. You must study in the gospel how Jesus brought his disciples to practise the truths of the gospel. . . .

In carrying out your service to children, you will not fulfill your ministry adequately if you conform only to the external actions of Jesus Christ in his guidance and in his conversion of souls. You must also enter into his way of thinking and adopt his goals. He came on earth, as he himself said, that all might have life and have it to the full. This is why he said in another place that his words are spirit and life. By this he meant that his words procure the true life, which is the life of the soul—for those who hear them and, with gladness over what they have heard, act on them with love. (*Meditations for the Time of Retreat*, pp. 57–58)

Reflection

In reaction to Martin Luther's emphasis on personal reading of the Bible, the Council of Trent discouraged laypeople from meditating on the word of God. Catholics were told to listen to the preaching of their priests, who would explain the Bible to them. The Catholic church placed stress on the role of tradition in informing the faithful as to the meaning of the sacred texts. Thus, De La Salle's exhortation to his Brothers to study the Gospels daily and to carry a copy with them at all times stood out as unusual in his era.

De La Salle's knowledge of scripture was profound. Passages from the Bible filled all of his meditations and other writings. He knew that by meditating on the word of God, people encounter Jesus Christ. Upon encountering Jesus, they will believe. In believing and in deepening this belief, they will be so filled with faith that they will spread the Good News effectively and live full lives.

✧ Pray slowly and meditatively this phrase: "O God, your words are spirit and life."

✧ Has a parable, story, or passage from the Bible been important to you in making a decision? Coping with a loss? Persevering in hard times? List some of your favorite stories from the Bible and recall how they have been spirit and life for you.

✧ A meditative studying of the Bible—*lectio divina*—is an ancient form of prayer for Christians. One way of doing *lectio divina* is this:

✦ Pick a short passage from a story or chapter in the Bible that strikes a chord with you.

✦ Read the passage slowly, relishing each word. Let God's Spirit speak to you through the words of the Scriptures you are reading.

✦ Ponder the passage, letting your mind wander over what you have read. A main idea will probably emerge, some notion that stands out because it relates to your life experience. Spend time thinking about these words; sometimes just repeating them over and over helps.

✦ Respond to the passage by talking to Jesus. Let the Spirit lead you. Express all your feelings and thoughts. (Many people like to write their responses or dialogs with Jesus in their journals.)

✦ End the meditation with a concluding prayer.

✧ If you are going to make the Gospels the first and principal rule of your life, you need to spend regular time with God's word. Is there some practical way in which you can spend time every day reading the Good News?

God's Word

Through [Jesus] you now have faith in God, who raised him from the dead and gave him glory for this very purpose—that your faith and hope should be in God.

Since by your obedience to the truth you have purified yourselves . . . , love each other intensely from the heart; for your new birth was not from any perishable seed but from imperishable seed, the living and enduring Word of God. . . . And this Word is the Good News that has been brought to you.

Rid yourselves, then, of all spite, deceit, hypocrisy, envy and carping criticism. Like new-born babies all your longing should be for milk—the unadulterated spiritual milk—which will help you to grow up to salvation, at any rate if you have tasted that the Lord is good. (1 Peter 1:21—2:3)

Closing prayer: God of all wisdom, may your words of truth and life be always on my lips and in my heart.

✧ **Meditation 3** ✧

Living in God's Presence

Theme: A principal help for growing in faith is to remind ourselves that God is always present with and in us. God's presence is a source of consolation and hope.

Opening prayer: Holy God, you are ever present.

About De La Salle

In a letter to a member of a religious community of women, De La Salle showed how simply being present to God is prayer and hopeful consolation:

> I realize, my dear Sister, that you are in great suffering and I deeply share in your difficulties; but you should not, it seems to me, grieve so much. Your feelings of abandonment touch only the exterior. The profound darkness which you experience is the means that God gives to draw you more surely to himself. You know quite well that the more darkness and doubt you experience in your life, the more you will live by faith; and you know that it is faith alone which should motivate the lives and actions of those who belong to God. Often say to yourself from the depths of your desolation, "Even if I become a reprobate, I will do all that I can for God." And if out of 20 actions, there is only one that is good or even

only partly good, still it will be so much done for love of God. . . . Once again I say, turn to God in prayer. Could doing this annoy him? Cast such a thought from your mind, dear Sister. I assure you that prayer always draws down some grace from God, even on the most hardened sinners. It is almost their only resort. And were you simply to remain in God's presence, that would still be a great help to you, supporting you in your troubles and helping you to bear them patiently. . . .

. . . Be sure that God is more ready than ever to welcome you into his arms, and that as your distress increases so does his mercy towards you increase and abound. (*Letters*, pp. 225–226)

Pause: Reflect on De La Salle's advice in this letter.

De La Salle's Words

Your sole concern . . . should be the establishment of God's reign in your heart, in this life and in the next. In this life your study should be to bring about this reign of God in your heart by His grace and through the plenitude of His love. You should live for God alone, and the life of your soul should be the life of God Himself. You ought likewise to nourish yourself with God by thinking of His holy presence as often as you possibly can. That which constitutes the life of the saints is precisely their continual attention to God, and this also should form the life of those who . . . seek only to accomplish His holy will, to love Him, and to make others love Him. (W. J. Battersby, ed., *De La Salle: Meditations*, p. 284)

We can consider God present in the place where we are because He is everywhere; and because, whenever two or three persons gather in Our Lord's name, He is in their midst. (P. 4)

[One consequence of living in the presence of God is] that all our actions will be referred to Jesus Christ and will tend towards Him as towards their center. They will draw all their vigor from Him. . . .

[Another consequence is] that He will pour out His Spirit upon us. . . . This same Holy Spirit will enliven our actions, and will become a lifegiving spirit in them. (John Baptist de La Salle, *Explanation of the Method of Mental Prayer*, p. 8)

Reflection

Meditating on the Scriptures nourishes our faith, but De La Salle also emphasized the practice of remembering God's presence. If God is with us, no one can overcome us. If we are acting in the presence of God, our actions will more likely reflect those of Jesus.

In his typically practical way, De La Salle mandated that in every classroom run by the Brothers, a bell should be rung every half hour and a student should say, "Let us remember that we are in the holy presence of God." He told his Brothers to kneel by their desks when they entered their classrooms, recall God's presence, and remind themselves that they stand on holy ground, just as Moses did at the burning bush. Using these and other practical measures, De La Salle hoped that the Brothers would teach with the wisdom and charity of Jesus.

On another level, paying simple attention to or resting alertly in God's presence is praying in a profound way. Despite our sinfulness, despair, doubt, and fears, God's love embraces us if we will only be present to the Creator and throw ourselves on God's mercy. To De La Salle, the God who is present is a God of tender care and infinite forgiveness.

✧ Prayer need not be talk. As De La Salle advised the troubled woman, resting in God's presence is often enough. Spend some time now resting in God's presence, listening rather than speaking. To help this process, sit comfortably. Perhaps play some quiet, meditative music. If you need to stretch stiff muscles, take some time and do so. Then plant your feet on the floor, rest your hands in your lap, close your eyes, and concentrate on deep, slow breathing. For a while, simply focus on your breathing. Then, for a while, pray one or two words that remind you that God is present with and in you (for example, "Jesus friend," "loving Spirit," "holy God"); as you breathe in, you might pray, "Jesus," and as you exhale slowly, pray, "friend." Do not feel compelled to keep praying the words. Just remain in God's healing presence until you feel refreshed.

✧ De La Salle suggested that we reflect on passages from the Bible:

> An easy means for making us more deeply aware of the presence of God, in an interior manner, is to recall some passage of Holy Scripture which will remind us of this presence, for example this one in Psalm 15:8. "I set the Lord ever in my sight.". . .
> . . . Through attention to some passage of faith joined with some simple reflections we can little by little acquire a certain facility for making ourselves aware of the presence of God by simple attention. (*Method of Mental Prayer,* pp. 24–25)

Spend some time praying with the scriptural passage in "God's Word" near the end of this meditation. Memorize one line that you may use to remind yourself of God's presence. Other useful passages to incorporate into your practice of perceiving God's presence are Genesis 17:1, Isaiah 6:3, Numbers 6:25, Matthew 28:20, and Acts 17:28.

✧ Another way of remembering God's presence is to recall that Jesus said, "Where two or three meet in my name, I am there among them" (Matthew 18:20). Reflect on this passage. Recall a meeting of friends or family in which you were conscious of God's presence. Then recall a time when a meeting with family and friends would have gone more smoothly and with more mutual caring if you had remembered God's presence in your midst.

✧ The Gospel of Luke says, "Look, the kingdom of God is among you" (17:21). Meditate on this passage. How can you celebrate the Kingdom of God among you?

✧ De La Salle knew that he had to build into his day definite ways of recalling God's presence. What practices can you establish to help you remember God's presence?

God's Word

Yahweh, you search me and know me.
You know if I am standing or sitting.
You perceive my thoughts from far away. . . .
Close behind and close in front you hem me in,
shielding me with your hand. . . .

If I flew to the point of sunrise—
or far across the sea—
your hand would still be guiding me. . . .
You created my inmost being
and knit me together in my mother's womb.
For all these mysteries—
for the wonder of myself,
for the wonder of your works—
I thank you. . . .

(Psalm 139)

Closing prayer: "I believe, O my God, that this place, whatever it may be, is a dwelling place for you. . . . You are in heaven; you are likewise on earth, which you permeate entirely. It contains you, but you rather contain it within yourself. This I believe, O my God, that wherever I go I shall find you, and that there is no spot not honored by your presence." (Adapted from De La Salle, *Method of Mental Prayer*, p. 32)

✧ **Meditation 4** ✧

Trusting in Providence

Theme: De La Salle believed that we are all held lovingly in God's hands. God provides.

Opening prayer: Loving God, present now and forever, teach me to rely on your providence.

About De La Salle

In the community in the rue Neuve which he [De La Salle] was so carefully fostering and to which he was now completely devoted, there developed an ominous movement. He noticed that the masters were once again growing restless under the severe restrictions and giving way to discouragement. Undoubtedly their life was a very hard one, and the death of one of their number the preceding May had come as a sharp reminder of the exhausting nature of their work in overcrowded class-rooms, and had perhaps alarmed them. But their chief complaint was that their future lacked security. After a life spent in arduous teaching they saw no prospect but the workhouse. In vain did De La Salle urge them to place their trust in God. . . . They answered that it was easy for him to talk, since he was in the comfortable enjoyment of a considerable fortune and the income from a canonry. He had nothing to fear. As for them, they were likely to be as poor after many years of hard work as they were when they began, if indeed they survived at all. . . .

De La Salle realized the force of these arguments and he concluded that the time had come for him to take the next step, which had been implicit in the first, namely to rid himself of his titles and wealth, and descend to the ranks of those of whom he was now the head. (Battersby, *De La Salle*, p. 52)

Soon after this incident, De La Salle gave his canonry to a poor parish priest and distributed all of his wealth to victims of the famine ravaging France at that time. Henceforth, he too had to rely on God's providence.

Pause: Reflect on how having the security of wealth insulates people from relying on God's providence.

De La Salle's Words

Although two years of famine [1684–1685] had gone by and although a large number of other people had lacked the necessities of life, his [De La Salle's] Community had always been provided for by the hand of their heavenly Father. Still, they were not without concern for the morrow. . . .

"Do not forget, my dear Brothers," he [De La Salle] told them, "the sad times we have just come through. You have seen with your own eyes all the calamities that famine brings down upon the poor and all the ravages it can occasion to the fortunes of the rich. This whole city was like one vast hospice where the poor in their destitution gathered and spent the last days of a life which hunger would soon close. During all this time, when the wealthiest were not always sure of finding, at whatever price, bread which had become as rare as it was expensive, what did you lack? Thanks be to God, although we have had neither money nor income, during these two terrible years, we have lacked nothing. We owe no one anything in any of our houses." (Canon John Baptist Blain, *The Life of John Baptist de La Salle*, book 1, p. 123)

Reflection

Reliance on divine providence means that we acknowledge our true position in God's creation. We depend on God for life. We are held in God's hands.

De La Salle relied on God's care-filled plan for him and for the Brothers. He came to realize that ownership and wealth would prevent him from making the bold moves necessary for his mission. Like the rich young man in the gospel story, De La Salle was challenged to give everything to poor people and follow Jesus. He freed himself from the protection of his inheritance and walked with Jesus, depending on him to provide.

That God sustains all things can be forgotten. As we invent better ways to protect ourselves from the elements, losing a sense of our vulnerability to natural forces becomes easier. Seeming to be able to control our environment more completely might lull us into a sense that we run our life and dictate our future.

When we experience a sudden loss of a loved one, when a hailstorm overtakes us in the open, when our health breaks down, or when we get older and realize that we do not have the energy we once did, we might remember that ultimately we do not run the universe. The loving God gives us what we need and sustains all things.

✧ Have certain events reminded you that you are completely dependent on God and that you do not order the universe? Recall some of these sharp reminders of your dependence on God. How did you feel about not being in control? Could you let go of the need for control? Converse with God about these times of dependence.

✧ Most of our life is filled with surprises. For instance, if we look at the things we have done over the last five, ten, or twenty years, few of us would have predicted that we could or would have done them.

Spend some time reflecting on the happy surprises God has provided in your life. Ponder the delightful ways in which God has provided for you, ways you would never have dreamed of years ago. Then make a litany of thanksgiving for these surprising gifts from the Provider; for instance, "Jesus, I never thought years ago that I was much good at making close friends, but now I have lots of them. Thank you!" or "Creator, I wouldn't have predicted that I'd enjoy being a parent and be much good at it. For the gift of parenthood, thank you!"

✧ De La Salle was hardly naive. He made sure that the people wanting the Brothers to open a school would be able to cover the expenses. On the other hand, he knew that money and property could be chains, preventing him from letting God lead him to the next challenge in his ministry.

Do you have any possessions that make demands on the energies you would like to spend in service to other people? Are there any ways in which you are controlled by what you own so that you cannot follow Jesus freely? Pray about any of these encumbrances.

✧ Go for a walk. Go camping, canoeing, or cycling. In other words, put yourself in a situation in which you can be affected by nature and over which you have no control. In prayer, acknowledge that God rules the universe.

✧ Part of God's providence is the family, friends, talents, and skills God gives us. Praise God for these gifts.

God's Word

Stop worrying so much about what your next meal will be, about how your body looks, or about dressing in fashion. Human life is more than food. Your body is worth more than the clothes draped on it. Watch the birds. Notice that they do not plant crops or store grain in silos, but the Creator gives them food. You are worth more than birds, aren't you? Can you add one second to your life by fretting about it? No. And why are you obsessed with clothing? The marvelous wildflowers do not sew or weave, but not even Solomon with all his wealth was arrayed as beautifully as a wildflower. So if God loves flowers so much, even though they wither and die in one season, don't you think the Creator loves you even more?

If you do not believe the Creator will take care of you, you do not have much faith. Stop worrying about everything so much. God knows what you need. Rather, turn your heart and focus your attention on building the Reign of God in your midst. These necessities will be given to you as well. Do not worry about tomorrow; tomorrow will fend for itself. Each day has sufficient trouble of its own. (Adapted from Matthew 6:25–34)

Closing prayer: God, grant me the courage to set my heart on building your reign and the faith to leave my fortunes in your loving care.

✧   **Meditation 5**   ✧

Discerning in All Things the Will of God

Theme: Christians are called to discern God's will by meditating on their experiences, reading the Scriptures, and seeking the advice of spiritual guides. Once we have used all means at our disposal to determine God's will, De La Salle urges us to go forward, trusting that God will help us.

Opening prayer: In your merciful presence, God, I ask you to open my heart and mind to your will in my regard.

About De La Salle

De La Salle and the Brothers were persistently harassed by the Guild of Writing Masters.

> He [De La Salle] was advised that the Christian schools in the parish of Saint Sulpice risked undergoing the same fate as those in the Faubourg Saint Antoine, since the writing masters apparently enjoyed complete liberty to cause the same disruption. . . . At the same time he was informed that those, on whose protection he had a right to count, were closing their eyes and affecting ignorance about the vexations carried out against the Brothers. . . .

. . . After having, so to speak, driven him out of Paris, they [the Writing Masters] wanted also to expel his Brothers from the city and wipe out the very name of the Christian and gratuitous schools.

. . . He [De La Salle] knew that men would strive in vain to overthrow his work if God protected it. . . .

"If my work," he declared, "does not come from God, I would consent to its ruin. I would join our enemies in destroying it if I thought that it did not have God for its author, or that He did not will its progress. But if He declares Himself its defender, let us fear nothing. He is the Almighty. No arm can uproot what He has planted; no hand can snatch away what He holds in His. . . . So, let us abandon ourselves to His guidance. If He takes our work in hand, He will make use of the very ones who are so determined to destroy it to further its progress. . . . If contradiction is a proof that an enterprise comes from God, let us be happy; our Institute is indeed His creation. The cross which follows it everywhere gives us assurance of this." (Blain, *De La Salle*, book 3, pp. 40–41)

Pause: Pray these words from De La Salle and ponder their meaning for you: "Let us abandon ourselves to His guidance."

De La Salle's Words

Indeed, if I had ever thought that the care I was taking of the schoolmasters out of pure charity would ever have made it my duty to live with them, I would have dropped the whole project. For since, naturally speaking, I considered the men whom I was obliged to employ in the schools at the beginning as being inferior to my valet, the mere thought that I would have to live with them would have been insupportable to me. Indeed, I experienced a great deal of unpleasantness when I first had them come to my house. This lasted two years.

It was undoubtedly for this reason that God, Who guides all things with wisdom and serenity, Whose way it is not to force the inclinations of persons, willed to commit me entirely to the development of the schools. He did this in an imperceptible way and over a long period of time so that one commitment led to another in a way that I did not foresee in the beginning. (Blain, *De La Salle,* book 1, p. 61)

Reflection

De La Salle relied on God's providence for support, but he realized that he was obliged to first seek and then do God's will. He never claimed to hear voices from heaven or to have direct revelations from God as to God's will for him. Instead, he searched for God's will by examining his experiences and the needs of God's people, by praying for enlightenment, by talking to spiritual directors and friends, and by poring over the Scriptures. Eventually, he would discover God's will.

Was he always sure that he was on the right track? No. Especially toward the end of his life, De La Salle seemed to suffer from doubts. When he had only one year to live, he wrote the following in a letter to Brother Barthélemy, who had been elected his successor as superior of the community:

I seriously think that, since I have given but little time to prayer for so long, it is right that I should now spend more time in prayer in order to learn what God wishes of me.

To my mind, what I must ask of God in prayer is that he tell me what he wants me to do and that he inspire me with the disposition he wants me to have. (*Letters,* p. 248)

De La Salle believed that God would indicate what he should do and that God would give him the will and power to do it.

✧ Select one line from the first two readings in this meditation and meditate on it. By repeating it in your mind, allow its meaning to become clearer.

✧ De La Salle outlines the following steps for discerning God's will. Use these steps for a meditation.

1. Think about some decisions that you need to make or some situations that are causing you confusion. Select only one decision or situation. Acknowledge that Jesus is with you now and explain to him all the facets of the decision or situation: the who, what, when, where, how, and why.

2. Listen to Jesus' response. One way of doing this is to recall biblical stories related to your situation. Another is to search the Gospels and the Epistles for the advice Jesus has for you. Each page is filled with infinite wisdom.

3. After you have listened to Jesus, talk with him some more in prayer.

4. If you need more clarity, discuss the decision or situation with someone you trust and who can help you.

5. Spend more time asking for the guidance of the Holy Spirit.

6. Decide, act, and monitor the results, knowing that God will help you.

7. If things go well, rejoice in your God. If the decision proves wrong or the situation cannot be resolved, trust that God is still with you and wishes you to grow in some way. Discern once again. God is merciful.

✧ God calls us in our ordinary experiences. To become more aware of God's call, look through the day's newspaper. Get a sense of what is going on in the world. Then spend some time praying over this question: Considering what is happening, are any of these events calling me to a new way of acting?

✧ Pray repeatedly these words of Jesus: "Let your will be done, not mine" (Luke 22:42).

God's Word

Thomas, the doubter, asked Jesus, "Since we don't know where you are going, how can we find you again?"

Jesus answered him: "I am the one true path. I am all truth. I am full life. People cannot approach God except through me. So, my friend, if you know me, then you know God too. Further, if you believe that I come from God, then you will do as I do, love as I love. You might even do greater works. And remember, if you ask anything from me, I will do it.

"Show your love for me by keeping my commandments. And to help you, I shall ask God to send you the Spirit of Truth to remain in your midst for all time. You will recognize the Spirit because the Spirit already lives in the core of your being. I will never leave you orphans. I will come to you." (Adapted from John 14:5–18)

Closing prayer: Loving God, send me your Spirit so that I too can say, believe, and act on these words spoken by De La Salle at the final moment of his life: "I adore in all things the designs of God in my regard" (*Collection*, p. 184). Amen.

✧ Meditation 6 ✧

Praying Always

Theme: De La Salle trusted the power of prayer. By turning his heart and mind to God, De La Salle received grace to overcome opposition, to teach the children well, and to accomplish God's will.

Opening prayer: Merciful God, grant that I may always pray in complete confidence that you will listen to my heart and provide what I need to be a more loving follower of your son.

About De La Salle

The Great Famine struck France in 1709. The Brothers ate a pound of black bread a day when they could find it. Many Brothers fell sick with scurvy and malnutrition; in the countryside, thousands of people died of starvation.

To add to his difficulties at this time, De La Salle received news that things were going amiss in Chartres. The Bishop, who held himself responsible for the upkeep of the Brothers, decided, for the sake of economy, to transfer the community residence from the parish of St. Hilary, where the Brothers were satisfactorily housed, to a large priory partly occupied already by the junior seminary. De La Salle informed the Director of Chartres by letter of His

Lordship's intentions. "He wishes to put us in St. Vincent's, where there is neither playground nor garden, which would be very inconvenient," he wrote. He then suggested what he thought ought to be done. "I think we should pray," he said, "and get the pupils to pray by making them continue the litanies, and that we should send two Brothers to Holy Communion every Sunday, every feast-day, and every Thursday half-holiday, in Our Lady's chapel in Notre-Dame Cathedral, to ask that His Lordship's plans be not carried out, and to obtain what is best for you in the matter of housing, and with regard to increasing the number of schools and pupils." Such was his characteristic method of opposing the designs of those in authority when he thought that those designs would be prejudicial to his work. . . . For his part, he intended to speak to the Bishop personally. (Battersby, *De La Salle*, p. 230)

Pause: Reflect on this story about De La Salle and his prayer.

De La Salle's Words

Be convinced of what St. Paul says, that you plant and water the seed, but it is God through Jesus Christ Who makes it grow, that He is the One Who brings your work to fulfillment. So, when you encounter some difficulty in the guidance of your disciples, when there are some who do not profit from your teaching and you observe a reckless spirit in them, turn to God with confidence. Earnestly ask Jesus Christ to make his Spirit come alive in you, since he has chosen you to do his work.

Consider Jesus Christ as the Good Shepherd of the gospel seeking the lost sheep, placing it upon his shoulders, and bringing it back to the fold. Since you are taking his place, look upon yourself as obliged to do the same thing. Ask him for the grace needed to bring about the conversion of the hearts of those in your care.

You must, then, devote yourself very thoroughly to prayer in order to succeed in your ministry. You must constantly represent the needs of your disciples to Jesus Christ, explaining to him the difficulties you experience in guiding them. Jesus Christ, seeing that you regard him as the one who can do everything and yourself as an instrument to be moved only by him, will not fail to grant you what you ask. (*Meditations for the Time of Retreat*, p. 56)

Reflection

De La Salle always connected prayer and work. The purpose of prayer, he said, is to seek "not repose but light to discover your faults, vices and passions, and the grace to correct them" (Battersby, *De La Salle*, p. 134). Prayer can help us order our life so that it becomes more like that of Jesus.

When De La Salle said that meditative prayer is not for seeking repose, he meant that prayer should not be used as an escape from reality. Rather, the calm that sometimes comes in meditation allows us to open our heart and mind to see ourselves clearly, our goodness and sinfulness, our weaknesses and our strengths. In repose, without being defensive, we can place ourselves in God's hands and ask for the grace to turn our life around. Prayer then feeds our faith and helps us discern God's will.

Prayer is often a conversation with God about our everyday experiences. For instance, De La Salle expected that asking God for guidance in working with troubled young people should be part of the prayer of the Brothers, and also of any parent or teacher. All topics are fit subjects for discussion with God, and a merciful God will always help.

De La Salle pointed out that conversations with God or meditation can turn to "simple attention," or contemplation, which he described as "an attitude of deep interior respect

[that] will lead the mind and heart to silent adoration, love, admiration, . . . and heartfelt desire to unite ourselves with [God]" (*Method of Mental Prayer*, p. 63). "Simple attention" cannot be worked at or learned. It is a gift from God that sometimes comes to people who regularly and conscientiously turn to God in prayer.

✧ Slowly read again the "About De La Salle" and "De La Salle's Words" sections in this meditation. Find one line that speaks to you in some special way. Pray the line, asking the Holy Spirit why it is important for you.

✧ Converse with Jesus about your prayer at this point in your life. What do you pray about? Who talks the most, you or God? How much time do you listen to the word of God? Do you spend enough time conversing with God about your experiences? Is there any topic you are ashamed to pray over? Do you ever express your joy in prayer?

If you keep a journal, you may want to write your dialog with Jesus about these questions.

✧ Take some time to vent your frustrations, anger, imbalance, worry, and desires to God. Tell God exactly how you feel about what is most negative in your life right now. You can open up with everything that you cannot tell anyone else. God can take it. Maybe in letting loose with God you can let loose yourself.

✧ A wonderful form of prayer is guided meditation. In the following prayer, you are led to a quiet spot in nature, there to encounter Jesus:

Close your eyes. . . . Relax. . . . Let all the tension go. . . . Breathe deeply in and out . . . in and out. . . . Feel the tensions leave your feet. . . . If you need to, tense your muscles and then just let them relax . . . now your legs. . . . Relax your stomach and chest. . . . Now let all the tensions escape from your arms . . . your neck. . . . Let your jaw and face relax, too. . . . Slow down . . . hear the breath of life flowing calmly in and out. . . .

Now see yourself walking slowly through a clearing in the woods. . . . Tall grass and wildflowers wave in the soft breeze, the sun caresses your face. . . . You stop to take in the scene: Birds flit among the flowers and fly into the pine trees ahead of you, butterflies float among the grass. . . . One stops near you. . . . You hardly breathe so that it won't wing away. . . . You breathe in and out deeply several times. . . . Slowly you walk on. . . .

A man sits on a log in the shade. . . . With a friendly wave, he invites you to share the log. . . . When you are close, he says, "Peace be with you.". . .

Your eyes are opened and you know that he is Jesus. . . . You look deeply into his eyes. . . . Jesus reaches out and takes your hand in his and says, "I love you with an everlasting love. . . . Now, my friend, tell me of the people you love. Share with me stories of those you love.". . .

See before you the faces of several people you love. . . . Tell Jesus about these loved ones. . . . Ask for the help or graces that they need. . . .

Jesus listens carefully. . . . When you are finished, he stands to go, saying, "Your sins are forgiven because you have loved much.". . . He embraces you. . . . Then you watch him as he walks slowly into the forest. . . .

When you are ready, return from the scene and open your eyes.

After this guided meditation, you might wish to write any reactions in your journal.

✧ Pray a litany of thanksgiving for all the gifts God has given you; for example, "For Steve's and Bob's friendship, I thank you, God," or "For a productive class, especially for Sara who is finally making progress, I thank you, God."

✧ Offer your petitions to Jesus, the Savior; for instance, "Help me support Tom's work, please Jesus," or "For Barb's safe trip to Philadelphia, please Jesus."

God's Word

So I say to you: Ask, and it will be given to you; search, and you will find; knock, and the door will be opened to you. For everyone who asks receives; everyone who searches finds; everyone who knocks will have the door opened. What father among you, if his son asked for a fish, would hand him a snake? Or if he asked for an egg, hand him a scorpion? If you then, evil as you are, know how to give your children what is good, how much more will [God] give the Holy Spirit to those who ask . . . ! (Luke 11:9–13)

Closing prayer: Complete your meditation by praying these words adapted from Luke 11:2–4:

God, Holy is your name,
may your Reign come;
give us each day the bread we need,
and forgive our sins,
for we forgive our sisters and brothers who are in our
    debt.
And do not put us to the test.

✧ Meditation 7 ✧

Owing Only Love

Theme: Christian love manifests itself in service to other people and in the treating of others and ourselves with forbearance and care. True love is not always glamorous, but it is always blessed.

Opening prayer: Loving God, create in me a loving heart so that I may be generous in my giving. Help me love my neighbors as I love myself.

About De La Salle

To De La Salle, charity needed to be taught to the children coming to the Brothers' schools. In his typically practical way, he gave these instructions to his followers in his manual for running Christian schools:

> The teachers should take care that the pupils bring with them every day their breakfast and lunch, and, without obliging them to do so, a little basket will be placed in an appointed place in the classroom, into which the children, when they are so piously inclined, may put what bread they have left over to be distributed among those of them who are poor. The teacher will see that they do not give away any of their bread unless they have enough left for themselves. Those who have bread to give

will raise their hands, showing at the same time the piece of bread which they have to give, and a pupil who has been appointed to receive these alms will go to get them. At the end of the meal, the teachers will distribute the bread to the poorest and will exhort them to pray to God for their benefactors. (*Conduct of the Schools*, p. 55)

Pause: Ponder this question: Is generous giving built into my lifestyle?

De La Salle's Words

For his meditation on the twentieth Sunday after Pentecost, De La Salle wrote about charity:

There are many . . . who wish to see miracles and wonders in their Brothers, in the sense that they would like to have to suffer nothing from them, which is a thing quite impossible. It is a law of God, and consequently an obligation on our part, that persons living together should exercise mutual forbearance. This is what St. Paul teaches when he says: "Bear the burden of one another's failings," that is to say their defects, "then you will be fulfilling the law of Christ.". . . To bear with the shortcomings of our neighbour is, moreover, a practice of charity which is essential to the preservation of union. Thus we show that we form but one body with our Brothers, and being one body we share in the sufferings of individual members. . . . It is impossible for two people to live together without being a source of mutual suffering, and as we cause others to suffer, it is but just that we should bear with their failings also. . . . And such a burden is light since Jesus Christ helps us to carry it.

Do not therefore be so lacking in sense, so unreasonable and so unchristian as to pretend that you should not have to suffer anything from your Brothers. This would truly be asking a most unheard of and extraordinary miracle. Do not expect to see any such thing during the whole of your life. (Battersby, *Meditations*, p. 309)

Reflection

De La Salle lived and worked with fallible human beings. Effective instructor that he was, he wanted to teach love of neighbor to the children and mutual tolerance to the Brothers.

De La Salle learned early on that children learn best through doing. So he built into his system of education a tangible way in which the children could help one another by sharing their food. He hoped that by both giving and receiving, his children would acquire the practice of love that would stay with them as adults.

Love demands forbearance. De La Salle's hardheaded realism about this may strike us as pessimistic, but he knew human beings. Living together, as the Brothers did, exposes the foibles and weaknesses of each person. People change only slowly, sometimes not at all. For the sake of union, bearing one another's burdens and failings is essential. Is this love? Certainly it requires love.

Love strives to foster the good of the other person in the context of the concrete situation. Giving bread is one way of loving, forbearing is another. De La Salle opened schools for poor children out of his love for them. He challenged his Brothers who doubted their abilities and consoled those who were hurt. Love takes many forms. In all ways of loving each other, we fulfill the law of Christ.

✧ Who has taught you charity? Reflect on the lessons you have learned about giving for the good of others. How well did you learn those early lessons? How would you evaluate your own commitment to living in a charitable way?

✧ De La Salle integrated opportunities for charity into the daily life of the school. Using the brief definition of *love* as "striving to foster the good of other people in their concrete situation," examine your actions of the last day or two.

List, mentally or in writing, each action that did good for someone. Leave nothing out, whether it was doing the laundry or guiding a new worker in your office. You may be doing more good than you are even conscious of.

Now thank God for each opportunity you had to show love for your neighbor.

Finally, meditate on this question: Can I build other acts of charity into my daily life?

✧ De La Salle was not passive in the face of evil. If he had been, he never would have begun schools and a community to run them. His pleas for forbearance reflect the sentiment of the Serenity Prayer: "God, grant me serenity to accept the things I cannot change, courage to change the things I can, and wisdom to know the difference."

Meditate on a relationship that is, right now, frayed or trying, but that you are committed to and want to grow. Sort through what aspects of the relationship you can help change and what aspects probably cannot change. Be as exact as possible in naming or describing the elements of your relationship. Finally, pray for the "wisdom to know the difference." Converse with God about this relationship.

✧ Pray a litany of thanksgiving for all the people who have cared for you and the people you love; for example, "For Aunt Margaret, who always encouraged me to read, I thank you God for her care," or "For Larry, a true friend, I thank you God."

✧ Pray for your enemies, people who do not wish to do you good.

✧ In unison with slow breathing, repeatedly pray the word "love." This is a prayer because God is love.

God's Word

Let love be without any pretence. . . . Let your feelings of deep affection for one another come to expression and regard others as more important than yourself. . . . Share with any of God's holy people who are in need; look for opportunities to be hospitable.

Bless your persecutors; never curse them, bless them. Rejoice with others when they rejoice, and be sad with those in sorrow. Give the same consideration to all others alike. Pay no regard to social standing, but meet humble people on their own terms. . . .

The only thing you should owe to anyone is love for one another, for to love the other person is to fulfil the law. All these: You shall not commit adultery, You shall not kill, You shall not steal, You shall not covet, and all the other commandments that there are, are summed up in this single phrase: You must love your neighbour as yourself. Love can cause no harm to your neighbour, and so love is the fulfilment of the Law. (Romans 12:9—13:10)

Closing prayer: "O my God, I love you with my whole heart, with my whole soul, and with all my strength, and above all things, because you are infinitely good, and worthy of being loved, and for the love of you I love my neighbor as myself." (Adapted from De La Salle, *Manual of Piety*, p. 11)

Creating Community

Theme: De La Salle drew the schoolmasters together into a community because he knew they would need the support, shared knowledge, and resources of people of like mind if they were to succeed in their mission.

Opening prayer: Jesus, be with me now as I meditate on the role of community in my life.

About De La Salle

One winter was so severe and one famine so deadly that the streets of Paris became perilous gauntlets for anyone carrying food.

> [De La Salle] took it upon himself to cater for the wants of his Brothers by going round to the houses of the wealthy and begging for help. "More than once," says Blain, "he was received in an ungracious manner, and was obliged to leave in shame and confusion.". . .
> . . . The Brothers suffered very severe hardships during this period of scarcity. . . . [They] were agreeably surprised one day to find that the larder, which was habitually bare, contained a piece of bread. It was only a very small piece and of very poor quality: *du pain noir*

[black bread]. But it was the result of much strenuous effort on the part of the one who was in charge of providing for the wants of the community, and was therefore handled with respect and accepted with gratitude. The joy of the Brothers was somewhat clouded with perplexity, however, when it came to dividing the bread among so many. De La Salle thought he had hit upon the solution by refusing to accept any, but this proved to be no solution at all, for nobody would touch it until he did. He therefore took a few crumbs and handed the rest round. Each Brother likewise took a very small quantity, after his example, with the result that, as in the Gospel narrative, there was some left over, although in this case it could hardly be said that everybody had had their fill. (Battersby, *De La Salle*, p. 126)

Pause: Reflect on this example of sharing.

De La Salle's Words

In his meditations on the Ascension, De La Salle wrote:

The third petition which Jesus makes to the Eternal Father for His Apostles . . . is that they should be closely united among themselves. This union should be so close and firm as to resemble that which exists between the three Divine Persons. . . . And this union of heart and mind which Jesus desires to see among His Apostles is to produce the same effect as the essential union between the Father, the Son and the Holy Ghost, that is to say, they are all to share the same sentiments, to have the same will, the same affections, the same rules and the same practices. . . . As St. Luke records in the Acts, saying, "there was one heart and soul in all the company of believers."

. . . Only by means of such harmony will you be able to maintain that peace which constitutes the whole happiness of your life. Ask therefore the Lord of all hearts to make yours one with those of your Brothers, in that of Jesus. (Battersby, *Meditations*, p. 174)

Reflection

The drive to create and experience community surges in every culture and in each individual. Common beliefs, rituals, and mores bond people into community. Christians are united by belief in the Triune God revealed in the life, death, and resurrection of Jesus Christ. This belief is expressed in communal liturgies and through shared values and common causes.

Community provides us with a sense of our identity and protects us. In the early days of Christianity, the followers of Jesus were known by their love for one another, expressed in their sharing of goods and care for one another.

De La Salle urged his followers to create community too. They should be united in sentiments, will, affections, rule, and practices. De La Salle believed that without community, his Brothers would become discouraged, lose their sense of mission, and drift away from their calling. He wanted the school to be a community as well, a place where the students found encouragement and guidance to lead lives that would create good in the church and in society. De La Salle's model for community was the Trinity itself—the three persons, each unique and distinct yet bonded together in love.

✧ Most of us belong to several communities. Consider the communities to which you belong, that is, the groups of people to whom you are united in affection, or will, or practice. Who are the members of your various communities? What do you do to actively build these communities?

✧ Do you feel a need to create community with a particular group of people? How do you experience this need? What beliefs, rituals, and values do you share that give focus to this community?

✧ In the "About De La Salle" section of this meditation, we see De La Salle and his Brothers sharing the little bread that they have. Another model of Christian community was given by Jesus at the Last Supper. He washed the feet of the Apostles, making them welcome and ready for the feast. He passed around the food, even to his betrayer, telling the Apostles to eat his body and drink his blood in remembrance of him.

Meditate on community using this guided imagery:

Sit relaxed. . . . Close your eyes. . . . Let all tension cease. . . . Begin with your feet; . . . feel the tension go. . . . Continue tensing and then relaxing each part of your body. . . . Meanwhile, breathe slowly and deeply. . . . Concentrate on your breathing for a while. . . .

Now imagine walking up stone stairs. . . . Darkness throws shadows on the stairs, but at the top is light flooding through an open door. . . . You step inside the door, and before you are twelve of your friends sitting at a table, all looking expectantly at Jesus. . . . He smiles at you and says, "Sit down at the table with us. Share our meal.". . .

Finding an empty chair, you sit. . . . Then Jesus takes out a pitcher of water, a bowl, and a towel. Starting at one end of the table, he washes each person's feet. . . . He comes to you . . . he smiles. . . . After you have removed your shoes, he washes and then dries your feet with the towel. . . . When he has gone around the table, he takes bread; blesses it, saying, "This is my body"; and then invites all of you to eat it. . . . He does the same with a cup of wine. . . . The room is silent as the sacred gifts are eaten and drunk. . . .

Finally, Jesus looks at you and asks, "My friend, you have shared our community. What can you do to create a loving community today, where you work, in your home, and in society? Tell me what you think.". . . You ponder his question, and then you tell him what you can do to build community. . . . When you finish, Jesus embraces you and says, "Go forth and create the reign of love on earth."

✧ Thank the loving God for the people with whom you are in community, the loved ones with whom you are united in affection, faith, and common cause.

✧ Action can be prayer. Is there some activity of your parish, family, or local community to which you could contribute your time, talents, and energy? Consider how you could take part.

God's Word

The whole group of believers was united, heart and soul; no one claimed private ownership of any possessions, as everything they owned was held in common.

The apostles continued to testify to the resurrection of the Lord Jesus with great power, and they were all accorded great respect.

None of their members was ever in want, as all those who owned land or houses would sell them, and bring the money from the sale of them, to present it to the apostles; it was then distributed to any who might be in need. (Acts 4:32–35)

These remained faithful to the teaching of the apostles, to the brotherhood, to the breaking of bread and to the prayers. (Acts 2:42)

Closing prayer: Complete your meditation by praying Psalm 133:

How good it is, how pleasant,
for God's people to live in unity.
It is like the precious oil
running down from Aaron's head and beard,
down to the collar of his robes.
It is like the dew on Mount Hermon
falling on the hills of Zion.
For there Yahweh has promised a blessing,
life that never ends.

Embracing the Poor

Theme: De La Salle saw the person of Jesus in the poor children to whom he ministered. He took seriously Jesus' warnings against having wealth when brothers and sisters lived in destitution.

Opening prayer: God of suffering and poor people, give me the courage and love to minister to your "little ones" and to allow them to minister to me. May we always have the necessities of life.

About De La Salle

De La Salle . . . now took the step which he had long premeditated of ridding himself of his inheritance. . . . Not only was it a barrier between himself and his community, as the Brothers themselves had pointed out, but it seemed to indicate a certain insincerity on his part in so far as it gave the lie to the humble garb which he had adopted for his community and which he had worn himself. . . . It was completely foreign to his nature to say one thing and do another; to preach what he did not practise. . . .

    . . . All he had to do, therefore, was to stand at the door of his house each day and distribute bread to those who wanted it. . . . The process continued until finally his wealth was gone. All he had left was a small sum of 200 *livres* which he had been advised to keep. . . .

His resources, in fact, were now gone, and he was obliged to face the hardships of real poverty in addition to the derision of his compatriots. It was no light matter. Brought up in comfortable circumstances, . . . he found it extremely difficult to accustom himself to the plain fare and severe conditions which he now, of necessity, had to accept. . . . But he refused to be treated differently. . . .

Thus, in poverty and self-abnegation, he settled down to his life's work. Like the athletes of old who stripped themselves for the race, he divested himself of all that could be a hindrance in the accomplishment of his mission. . . . In a word, he was free. (Battersby, *De La Salle*, pp. 65–69)

Pause: Ask yourself if you need to divest yourself of any hindrances to following Jesus' call to you.

De La Salle's Words

De La Salle wrote this meditation on the Feast of the Adoration of the Magi:

The Magi entered the poor hamlet of Bethlehem in search of the King they were looking for. . . .

How is it that at this sight the Magi did not fear to have been mistaken? Are these the marks of royalty, asks St. Bernard? Where are His palace, His throne and His court? . . . This stable did not appear to them despicable; those swaddling clothes did not shock them; and they took no exception to the sight of a poor Child being suckled by His mother. "They fell down to worship Him," says the gospel. They respected Him as their King, and adored Him as their God. That is what the faith with which their mind was enlightened led them to do.

You should learn to recognize Jesus beneath the rags of the poor children whom you have to teach. Adore Him in their person. Cherish poverty and honour the poor, after the example of the Magi, for poverty should be amiable in your eyes since you are engaged in instructing the poor. Faith should lead you to acquit yourself of this task with zeal and affection, since the poor are the members of Christ, . . . for He always loved poverty and the poor. (Battersby, *Meditations*, p. 40)

Reflection

De La Salle told the Brothers to love poor people and a simple life. Poor people deserve respect, justice, and care. He established the schools to enable children to escape spiritual and physical poverty, and the crime and despair that it spawned.

On the other hand, De La Salle knew that wealth is not the end of human life; union with God is. He was concerned that people needed to free themselves from wealth in order to focus their life on union with God. By emptying themselves of the "world," they can be filled with God. De La Salle called us to divest ourselves of anything that would prevent the complete gift of ourselves to God and to love of our neighbor.

Jesus was born poor. He had nowhere to call home. In his poverty, he showed us that ultimately all of us must rely on God's goodwill. The power of wealth seduces people into believing that they control their destiny. Poor people tend to have no such illusions. They are more likely to acknowledge their dependence on God and to turn to God for help.

So De La Salle challenges us to serve God's "powerless ones," the *anawim*; to live simply; to give generously; and to see Jesus in the faces of poor and needy people. If we are poor and struggling to make ends meet, it is hoped that we will have the integrity of a child of God and that when we look in the mirror, we can see in our face the face of Jesus.

✧ Look through today's newspaper. Find articles and pictures of God's poor and suffering people. Slowly read the articles, or meditatively study the faces of the people. Then repeat as a prayer this phrase from the preceding "De La Salle's Words": "The poor are the members of [the Body of] Christ." If you are having a hard time financially, pray, "I am a member of the Body of Christ."

✧ Fast or abstain one day this week. In your want, remember hungry people. Pray for them, and ponder how your way of life might contribute to unjust systems that perpetuate poverty. Set aside the money you saved on food purchases and contribute it to a local food shelf.

✧ De La Salle remarked, "Our Brothers will survive so long as they are poor. They will lose the spirit of their vocation as soon as they start procuring for themselves the unnecessary commodities of life" (Blain, *De La Salle*, book 1, p. 124). Does this admonition hold true for all Christians? Can we hold fast to our vocation or calling to be Christlike if we start building up treasures and forgetting the needs of poor people?

✧ As a form of prayer, sort through your clothes, setting aside seldom-used or superfluous items. Clean and fold these garments. Pray for the poor people who can use them, and then donate them to an agency that serves poor people.

✧ Meditate on how you might respond more fully to the Christian call to justice.

God's Word

Listen . . . : it was those who were poor according to the world that God chose, to be rich in faith and to be the heirs to the kingdom. . . . You, on the other hand, have dishonoured the poor. Is it not the rich who lord it over you? Are not they the ones who drag you into court, who insult the honourable name which has been pronounced over you? Well, the right thing to do is to keep the supreme Law of scripture: you will love your neighbour as yourself. (James 2:5–8)

Closing prayer: Jesus, may I embrace the simplicity of lifestyle that you chose. Help me to give cheerfully and generously and to respect the dignity of people who are poor, suffering, or oppressed. Finally, may I value myself as a child of God rather than for what I own or how much I have in the bank.

✧ Meditation 10 ✧

The Body of Christ

Theme: De La Salle believed that unity in the church was best symbolized by the successor to Peter, the bishop of Rome. He concluded that the Body of Christ is best served when people hold firmly to their faith.

Opening prayer: Jesus, you formed the church to spread the Good News and to be a loving community. May I commit myself to building up your Body.

About De La Salle

During De La Salle's life, the Jansenist heresy flourished in France. Jansenists held that human nature was intrinsically corrupted by original sin and that Christ died only for those predestined to go to heaven. The pope condemned the heresy, but the cardinal archbishop of Paris and others in France refused to recognize his position. To De La Salle's deep regret, his own brother Louis sided with the Jansenists. The two split over this issue, with John Baptist remaining staunch in his support of the church.

A list of names of Jansenist sympathizers was drawn up and circulated in the diocese [of Boulogne], and [John Baptist] De La Salle's name was included. When this came to his knowledge it drew from him an indignant

76

protest, and on January 28th, 1719, he sent this letter to the Director of the Calais community.

"My dear Brother, I do not think I have given occasion to the Reverend Dean to say that I am one of the appellants to a future Council. I have too much respect for our holy Father the Pope, and too great a submission to the decisions of the Holy See, to acquiesce in such a thing. I wish in this matter to imitate St. Jerome, who, on the occasion of a difficulty in the Church caused by the Arians, who required him to admit the existence of three hypostases in God, thought it his duty to consult the Chair of Peter, upon which, he said, he knew the Church was built. . . .

"Neither the Reverend Dean nor anyone else should be surprised, therefore, if I, following the example of this great saint who was so enlightened in matters of religion, should declare that it suffices me to know that he who today sits in the Chair of St. Peter has condemned by a Bull, accepted by almost all the bishops of the world, one hundred and one propositions from the book of Father Quesnel [the leading theorist of Jansenism], and if, after such an authentic decision of the Church, I should say with St. Augustine that the case is ended. Such is my sentiment in this matter and my disposition; it has never been anything else and I shall never change it."

It is hardly surprising that such an uncompromising attitude should have created enemies both for himself and his Brothers in the diocese of Boulogne. (Battersby, *De La Salle*, p. 281)

Pause: Reflect on your reactions to De La Salle's submission to the Chair of Saint Peter.

De La Salle's Words

For the Feast of Saint Peter, De La Salle wrote this meditation:

> We must not be astonished if St. Peter was so greatly loved by Our Lord, and if he was appointed by Him to be Head of the Church. It was because of his great faith that he received this honour; a faith that led him to leave all things to follow Christ. . . .
>
> The result of St. Peter's great faith was that he always followed Jesus Christ, and of the three Apostles who accompanied Our Lord in the principal events of His life, Peter is always named first in the gospel. He was the first of the twelve to go to the tomb to look for the Body of his beloved Master; a fact which testifies to his great love for Christ. His faith shone far more vividly than that of the other Apostles. . . . As a reward for this, Our Lord entrusted him with the care of the Church.
>
> Rest assured that you will do good in the Church only in so far as you are filled with faith, and conduct yourself by the Spirit of Faith. (Battersby, *Meditations*, pp. 546–547)

Reflection

De La Salle's loyalty to papal authority may strike us as too servile, but it becomes more understandable in the light of the church's situation in seventeenth-century France.

For centuries, the French church enjoyed considerable autonomy from the papacy. The king appointed bishops and other church officials, who, in turn, became extensions of the state regime. While many churchpeople devoted themselves to their ministry and to being models for their community, many others became absentee bishops who spent more time at court than in their diocese. De La Salle respected the dignity of bishops. However, given his own dedication to the service of poor children and to living a virtuous life, he showed little concern for power and more for adherence to the true faith and church traditions that he perceived were protected by the papacy.

He held Peter up as a model, not because he considered Peter to be the first bishop of Rome, but because Peter held fast to his belief in Jesus. De La Salle wanted his Brothers to live by a faith promoted and protected when in union with Peter's successors. This firm faith would inspire the Brothers to stick to the challenging task of teaching poor children and to cope cheerfully with their Spartan lifestyle.

✧ How would you evaluate your relationship with the church? Spend some time in an examination of consciousness, using these questions:

✦ In what activities of my local church am I involved?

✦ Are my needs as a believer being met by my congregation?

✦ Do I find Sunday celebrations and other liturgies meaningful?

✦ Are there ways in which I could become more involved?

✦ What are my biggest questions or criticisms of the international church?

✦ What are the aspects of belonging to the church that nourish my life and attract me?

If writing your responses helps you, consider doing so.

✧ If you feel a need for some reconciliation of your feelings about the church, this meditation may help:

First, relax. Get comfortable. Reach back into your memory, and recall one or two incidents when you were hurt by the church or by a person in the church. When you have clearly pictured the incident, allow yourself to enter the next part of this meditation.

With your eyes closed, recall the setting, the incident, the hurtful words. . . . Imagine Jesus present in that scene, understanding your point of view and the other person's point of view. . . . Listen to what Jesus says to you. . . . Listen to what Jesus says to the other person. . . . Ask Jesus to help you understand each other and to lead you to some act that expresses your reconciliation. . . .

Now recall a time when you were hurtful to the church or to a person in the church. . . . Invite Jesus into the scene.

. . . Tell him why and how you were hurtful. . . . Ask him for forgiveness and for ways of reconciling yourself with the church.

✧ Ask God to aid the church. Then, thank God for the ways in which the church serves, spreads the Good News, and worships.

God's Word

So, . . . keep firm and immovable, always abounding in energy for the Lord's work, being sure that in the Lord none of your labours is wasted.

Now about the collection for God's holy people; you are to do the same as I prescribed for the churches in Galatia. On the first day of the week, each of you should put aside and reserve as much as each can spare; do not delay the collection till I arrive. When I come, I will send to Jerusalem with letters of introduction those people you approve to deliver your gift; if it is worth my going too, they can travel with me.

In any case, I shall be coming to you after I have passed through Macedonia . . . and I may be staying some time with you. . . .

If Timothy comes, make sure that he has nothing to fear from you; he is doing the Lord's work, just as I am, and nobody is to underrate him. Start him off in peace on his journey to come on to me: the brothers and I are waiting for him. . . .

Be vigilant, stay firm in the faith, be brave and strong. Let everything you do be done in love. . . .

The churches of Asia send their greetings. Aquila and Prisca send their best wishes in the Lord, together with the church that meets in their house. All the brothers send their greetings. Greet one another with the holy kiss.

This greeting is in my own hand—PAUL. . . .

My love is with you all in Christ Jesus. (1 Corinthians 15:58—16:24)

Closing prayer: Complete your meditation by praying these words from Psalm 84:

How I love your dwelling place,
Yahweh Sabaoth!
How my soul yearns and pines for your courts!
My heart and my flesh cry out to you, the living God. . . .
Happy those who dwell in your house
and praise you all day long.
Happy those whose strength is in you;
they have courage to make the pilgrimage! . . .
Yahweh Sabaoth, happy those who put their trust in you.

✧ **Meditation 11** ✧

Many Ministries, the Same Spirit

Theme: De La Salle truly believed that God calls each person to minister to the People of God in different ways and that salvation is found in each person's ministry. We should embrace the ministry God calls us to, no matter how humble it seems.

Opening prayer: Holy Spirit, living within me and within all of God's Creation, grant that I may understand more completely the ways in which you are calling me to minister to my neighbors.

About De La Salle

De La Salle learned about his ministry and the ministry of the Brothers through the experiences of his life and their life together. He believed that the community of Brothers would gain credibility in the eyes of society and the church if its superior were a priest. So he sent Brother Henri l'Heureux to study for ordination. Brother Henri, who seemed in perfect health, died suddenly.

The news broke his [De La Salle's] heart. . . . This first movement of human grief was followed by a deeply religious reaction and resignation to God's holy will. He adored His eternal designs, and declared on the spot that the sudden demise of Brother Henri was a warning from Heaven, indicating that the Institute should not include priests among its members. . . .

. . . In a word, the Brothers chosen and given preference for promotion to Sacred Orders would not be slow in preferring themselves to the others, in trying to dominate them, in losing esteem for their vocation and the spirit that should characterize it, along with the grace of their state. . . .

Would such priest-Brothers be humble enough to confine themselves to the limitations of a vocation which has nothing flamboyant about it in the world's eyes, nothing to flatter self-love? Would they restrict themselves to the role of the schoolmaster, and to the useful and necessary function of teaching catechism simply . . . ? (Blain, *De La Salle*, book 2, pp. 95–96)

Pause: Reflect on De La Salle's belief that each state in life has its own grace.

De La Salle's Words

God is so good that He not only brings us into existence by His act of creation but also desires that all of us come to the knowledge of truth. This truth is God Himself and all that He has willed to reveal to us through Jesus Christ, through His apostles, and through His church. God desires all of us to be taught this knowledge, that our minds may be enlightened by the light of faith.

We cannot be taught the mysteries of our religion unless we have the good fortune to hear about them, and we cannot have this advantage unless someone preaches the word of God. . . .

God diffuses the fragrance of His knowledge throughout the world by human ministers. Just as He commanded light to shine out of darkness, so He also kindles a light in the hearts of those whom He has called to announce His word to children, to enlighten them by making the glory of God known to them.

Since God in His mercy has given you such a ministry, do not falsify His word but gain glory before Him by proclaiming His truth to those whom you are called to teach. Let this be your continual effort in the lessons you give them, looking upon yourselves as the ministers of God and the administrators of His mysteries. (*Meditations for the Time of Retreat*, p. 47)

Reflection

Educating wealthy young people had been done in monasteries and in other schools, but teaching poor children at the elementary level was viewed as beneath male religious congregations. By working in charity schools, De La Salle elevated teaching in poor schools to a genuine ministry and, in effect, created a new form of ministry for laypeople.

Permeated by the spirit of the Scriptures, De La Salle recognized that every activity is Christian ministry that leads to human wholeness, that serves to heal the brokenness among God's people, whether it be loneliness, poverty, powerlessness, ignorance, injustice, or physical or emotional pain. The Spirit calls us to ministry and provides the gifts to accomplish it. Furthermore, as we minister, we make Christ, the suffering servant of God, present in the world.

✧ In the Christian Testament, ministries may be roughly grouped as of the word (*kerygma*), community building (*koinonia*), celebration (*leitourgia*), or serving and healing (*diakonia*).

✦ Which of these ministries do you find most compatible with your abilities? Why?

✦ How are you making Christ, the suffering servant, present in the world? By offering hospitality? By directly serving people? By nurturing your family? By practicing stewardship of the environment?

✧ Another way of appreciating your own gifts as a minister is to ask yourself how you are the following:

✦ Hands of Jesus to people . . .
✦ Voice of Jesus . . .
✦ Ears of Jesus . . .
✦ Eyes of Jesus . . .
✦ Body of Jesus . . .

✧ Ask the Holy Spirit for the graces you need to be God's minister in whatever work you do or lifestyle you lead.

God's Word

For what is Apollos and what is Paul? The servants through whom you came to believe, and each has only what the Lord has given him. I did the planting, Apollos did the watering, but God gave growth. In this, neither the planter nor the waterer counts for anything; only God, who gives growth. It is all one who does the planting and who does the watering, and each will have the proper pay for the work that he has done. After all, we do share in God's work; you are God's farm, God's building.

By the grace of God which was given to me, I laid the foundations like a trained master-builder, and someone else is building on them. . . . For nobody can lay down any other foundation than the one which is there already, namely Jesus Christ. On this foundation, different people may build in gold, silver, jewels, wood, hay or straw but each person's handiwork will be shown for what it is. The Day which dawns in fire will make it clear and the fire itself will test the quality of each person's work. . . .

Do you not realise that you are a temple of God with the Spirit of God living in you? If anybody should destroy the temple of God, God will destroy that person, because God's temple is holy; and you are that temple. (1 Corinthians 3:5–17)

Closing prayer: May I remain conscious of your caring presence, my holy friend, Spirit of God. Empower me to minister to your world in ways suitable to my talents and my call from you.

The Person of the Teacher

Theme: If the Good News is to be heard and believed, it must be proclaimed by persons who have put on Jesus Christ themselves. Although De La Salle wrote specifically for his Brothers, his words apply to all Christians since all are called to spread God's word.

Opening prayer: Brother Jesus, help me to grow more and more like you, in heart, mind, and action, so that I can be an effective teacher of your word.

About De La Salle

De La Salle's correspondence often reflected his attitudes about the conduct of the teacher that is best suited to bring students to God. Indeed, De La Salle wanted his Brothers to put on Jesus Christ, but he also knew that they were sorely tested and only human.

Letter to Brother Denis, July 8, 1708
Conclude conversations briefly with persons who come to the school door in order not to let the pupils waste time.

Be careful to correct the children, the ignorant even more than the others.

It is disgraceful to call them hurtful names. Be careful not to let human respect prevent you from doing good. It is really disgraceful to call your pupils by insulting names, and it also gives them bad example. . . .

Keep an eye on that Brother who slaps the students and see to it that he stops doing it. This is most important. (*Letters*, pp. 25–27)

Letter to Brother Hubert (at age 23, director of a school),
June 1, 1706
When you feel yourself giving way to impatience in class, remain still and silent for a short time until the feeling has passed. (*Letters*, p. 36)

Letter to Brother Robert, December 7, 1708
Take care not to let yourself give way to impatience and to outbursts of anger. . . .

It is better to omit some part of the spiritual exercises than to take time from class to carry out what is necessary, for you must not lose a minute from class. . . .

Make sure you don't reduce the numbers of the students by your rebuffs, but teach them well so that they will not leave.

You must not take them on to a new lesson before they are ready. Be careful about this, otherwise they will learn nothing. (*Letters*, p. 142)

Letter to the same Brother Robert, April 26, 1709
Make sure that you keep an even disposition in class, and don't give way to impatience. It is not good to throw the ferule at the students in class, but it is disgraceful to slap them, especially in church.

It is good to know that you have a large number of students. Be sure to see that they make good progress. (*Letters*, p. 147)

Pause: Can you identify with the problems that these teachers had?

De La Salle's Words

Since you are ambassadors and ministers of Jesus Christ in the work that you do, you must act as representing Jesus Christ himself. He wants your disciples to see him in you and receive your teaching as if he were teaching them. They must be convinced that the truth of Jesus Christ comes from your mouth, that it is only in his name that you teach, that he has given you authority over them.

They are a letter which Christ dictates to you, which you write each day in their hearts, not with ink, but by the Spirit of the living God. For the Spirit acts in you and by you through the power of Jesus Christ. (P. 54)

. . . Your zeal for the children under your guidance would be very imperfect, if you expressed it only in teaching them; it will only become perfect if you practise yourself what you are teaching them. Example makes a much greater impression on the mind and heart than words. This is especially true of children, since they do not yet have sufficient capacity for reflection, and ordinarily model themselves on the example of their teachers. They are led more readily to do what they see done for them than to carry out what they hear told to them, particularly when the words they hear are not in harmony with the actions they see. (*Meditations for the Time of Retreat*, p. 80)

Reflection

Great, Christ-filled teachers, mentors, or parent figures are special kinds of people. If we think of our best teachers, we remember them not only for what they knew, not just for what techniques they used, not solely for their dedication or kindness, but for who they were as persons.

De La Salle formed the ragged band of schoolmasters into a religious community of Brothers because he realized that unless these men became more Christ-filled themselves, they could hardly be expected to pass on to children the Good

News of Jesus. Every study done about the learning of values and religion indicates the same conclusion De La Salle came to.

All adult Christians, but especially parents and teachers, are called to become other-Christs to children. For this reason, De La Salle constantly reminded his Brothers to be patient, to treat the children with respect, or to avoid the sort of personal attack that would turn the children's heart away from learning and from God.

✧ Read the "About De La Salle" section of this meditation again. Select the comment by De La Salle that most applies to you and reflect on it. Then converse with Jesus about ways you can be more like him in this regard.

✧ If you need to remind yourself of your role in spreading God's word, pray repeatedly and meditatively these words: "I am an ambassador and minister of Jesus Christ."

✧ Ponder your relationships with your children, or your students, or any young people with whom you interact. How would you characterize the ways you deal with them? In what ways could you be more like Jesus in your relationships with them? Ask God for the graces you need to be a more Christlike example to them.

✧ Make a list of five people who have been powerfully good influences in your life—your most important teachers, mentors, or parent figures. Think of the qualities they possessed that made them Christlike. Then select the one person who has had the most profoundly good influence on you. Bring to mind some incidents, like conversations or visits, that you shared with this person. Let your imagination recall these times in vivid detail.

Have you acted toward any other people as this person acted toward you? Reflect on ways in which you have ministered to other people as this special person ministered to you.

✧ Thank God for each of your teachers, mentors, or parent figures. Lift up their names and your fond memories of them to God.

God's Word

Ask yourself, can a blind person guide another blind person? They will both stumble into trouble. Students are not above their teachers, even though someday, with proper training, they may be peers. So why do you always seem to point out the sliver in someone else's eye, but never notice that you have a ten-foot beam in your own? You cannot be much help to the person with the sliver, if you cannot even see the beam blinding you. Do not be such a hypocrite. Rid your eye of the beam. Then, with clear vision, you can remove the sliver from your neighbor's eye.

Rotten fruit does not grow on healthy trees. Healthy fruit does not grow on rotten trees. You know the quality of the tree by the fruit it bears. A good life is nourished by the reservoir of goodness in the heart of the good person. Evil people exist on the evil in their heart. Our words flow out of what is in our heart. (Adapted from Luke 6:39–45)

Closing prayer: "You, my God, are my strength, my patience, my light, and my counsel; it is you who opens the minds and hearts of the children confided to my care. Abandon me not to myself for one moment. For my own conduct and for that of my pupils, grant me the spirit of wisdom and understanding, the spirit of counsel and fortitude, the spirit of knowledge and piety, the spirit of holy fear of you, and an ardent zeal, to procure your glory. Amen." (Adapted from De La Salle, "Prayer of the Master Before School," *Manual of Piety*, p. 72)

✧ **Meditation 13** ✧

The Manner
of Christian Teaching

Theme: To teach the word of God effectively requires good example from teachers, but the manner and methods of teaching are also important.

Opening prayer: Come Holy Spirit, descend upon us and sanctify us. Replenish our heart with your holy grace, and light in us the fire of your love. Confirm us in faith and in our union with you so that we may teach as Jesus did.

About De La Salle

Although he [De La Salle] placed the teaching of religion and the training of the pupils in piety first in importance in his schools, he by no means neglected the other subjects of the curriculum. But the question which confronted him was how best to do this with the large numbers of boys who swarmed to his classes. He spent hours each day in the badly ventilated, overcrowded rooms, observing his teachers and thinking out the most advantageous system to adopt. The individual method, . . . where the teacher had only a handful of pupils, was out of the question. . . . The class, he thought, would have to be treated as one unit, with subdivisions according to the ability of the pupils, and with one Brother instructing the whole group.

In this way he came to adopt the simultaneous or class method of teaching which has since become universal. In this matter he has been hailed as a pioneer, but he was not posing as an inventor of new methods in education, or seeking a reputation for reviving and popularizing an old neglected system. He was merely the slave of necessity. Nor was he blind to the dangers inherent in a system where the individual tends to be obliterated in the mass. He warned his Brothers against it, and endeavoured to assure as much individual attention to each pupil as he possibly could. In one of his Meditations he wrote: "One of the essential qualities required of those who instruct others is that they must know their pupils, and discern the manner in which to act towards them." (Battersby, *De La Salle*, pp. 103–104)

Pause: Ponder the importance of first knowing other people in order to care for them well.

De La Salle's Words

Jesus compares those who have care of souls to a good shepherd who is very careful of his sheep. One of the qualities which Our Lord says distinguishes him is that he knows them all individually. This is also one of the essential qualities required of those who instruct others, for they must get to know their pupils, and discern the manner in which to act towards them. Some require great mildness, while others need to be directed with firmness. Some require much patience; others need to be goaded on. . . . This varied conduct must depend upon knowledge and discernment of character, and this grace you must beg of God most earnestly, as being one of the most essential for you in the direction of those over whom you have charge. (P. 148)

Have you . . . charity and tenderness towards the poor children whom you have to instruct? Do you avail yourself of the affection the children have for you to attract them to God? If you show the firmness of a father in withdrawing them from evil, you should also show the tenderness of a mother in gathering them together, and in doing them all the good in your power. (Battersby, *Meditations*, p. 400)

Reflection

The law of God prompts Christians to love their neighbors as they love themselves. Love implies seeking to foster the good of other people in their real circumstances. Thus, effective teaching or Christian service should begin by identifying the genuine needs of those served.

God sees us as we are—one person at a time—not en masse. The plan of God manifests itself in an individualized way. Consequently, God calls us to see and to serve each unique child of God by expressing love in the ways needed by that child.

Because the children had to get the most out of school in a short time, De La Salle's Brothers taught in the children's native language instead of in Latin. De La Salle employed the best means, the simultaneous method, by which to teach the crowds of children. Even so, he still recognized and established procedures to nurture the uniqueness of each child.

De La Salle's methods struck many of his critics as improper, but criticism did not stop him. His love for God's poor children freed him to do what was best, not just what was common practice.

✧ Most of us are familiar with charitable works that have gone sour because the genuine needs of those to be served had not been studied first. Charity for individual people can go amiss for the same reason, lack of knowledge. Love requires knowledge—of the other people, their needs, their circumstances, and so on.

Reflect on one of your relationships, perhaps one blocked by some difficulty. Then, remembering the wise Spirit within you, consider the other person's personality, problems, virtues, quirks, and situation. Meditate on ways to love that other person, taking into consideration her or his genuine situation. This can be what De La Salle called "discernment of character."

✧ De La Salle unabashedly said that teachers should have affection for students. He would not accept Christian teachers' distancing themselves from their students as being proper. In turn, he saw that a child's affection for the teacher can draw the child to God.

Converse with Jesus about your own way of being affectionate to your students, or children, or patients, or co-workers. Do you ever experience fear of showing affection? Talk to Jesus about the role of affection in your ministry.

✧ Pray for individual students, children, or persons with whom you work. Ask God's help in knowing how best to love each one. In addition, thank God for each one and the gifts that each gives to you.

God's Word

You are all children of light and children of the day: we do not belong to the night or to darkness, so we should not go on sleeping, as everyone else does, but stay wide awake and sober. . . . Let us put on faith and love for a breastplate, and the hope of salvation for a helmet. God destined us . . . to win salvation through our Lord Jesus Christ, who died for us. . . . So give encouragement to each other, and keep strengthening one another, as you do already. . . .

Be at peace among yourselves. We urge you . . . to admonish those who are undisciplined, encourage the apprehensive, support the weak and be patient with everyone. Make sure that people do not try to repay evil for evil; always aim at what is best for each other and for everyone. Always be joyful; pray constantly; and for all things give thanks; this is the will of God for you in Christ Jesus.

Do not stifle the Spirit. (1 Thessalonians 5:5–19)

Closing prayer: "Jesus, the perfect teacher, live in my heart through faith so that I may grow firm in my inner self. Then, rooted in love, I will have the strength to grasp the breadth and the length, the height and the depth; so that, knowing your love, which is beyond knowledge, I may be filled with the utter fullness of God. Glory be to you whose power, working in me, can do infinitely more than I can ask or imagine. Amen." (Adapted from Ephesians 3:14–21)

Perseverance

Theme: Despite enormous odds against him, De La Salle persevered in his mission because of his profound faith and love. God provided, and De La Salle held fast, realizing that he would never accomplish anything on his own.

Opening prayer: I place my trust in you, faithful God. In times of trouble, help me persevere on the path of truth and life. I trust that you are now upholding me.

About De La Salle

Some of his friends, also, came to St. Yon to see him, and keep him informed as to the progress of his work in other towns. Two such persons were Mr. Gense of Calais, and Mr. de La Cocherie of Boulogne. In the company of these worthy gentlemen, who had spent their lives in charitable works and had devoted much of their wealth to the same purpose, he felt at ease, and spoke more freely than to most. When the subject turned on the question how he came to take up the task of educating the poor, he said:

"I tell you, gentlemen, that if God, in showing me the good that would be done by this Society had also discovered to me the trials and crosses which were to accompany it, I would have lacked courage, and far from assuming charge of it, I would not have dared to touch it with the tips of my fingers. Meeting constantly with opposition, I have been persecuted by several prelates, even by those from whom I expected help. My own spiritual children, whom I had tenderly cherished and trained with the greatest care, and from whom I expected the most valuable services, have risen against me, and have added interior trials, the most bitter of all, to my exterior crosses. In a word, if God had not stretched out His hand to sustain this edifice in a visible manner, it would long since have been buried in ruins." (Battersby, *De La Salle*, p. 269)

Pause: Reflect on how God has sustained you in times of trial.

De La Salle's Words

De La Salle wrote this meditation for the fourth Sunday in Lent:

When, in your troubles, you have had recourse to those who conduct you and they have been unable to supply the appropriate remedy, God requires that you should remain in a state of entire abandonment to His good pleasure, awaiting from His goodness the help you need, after the example of the multitude of people who had followed Our Lord and who waited patiently for Him to supply their wants without even troubling to expose them. You may, in fact, rest assured that God will not allow you to be tried beyond your strength. It is when men are powerless that He does all, and thereby manifests His power and goodness in a striking manner.

Hence, like those people who followed Christ, you must confide in God to suffer so long as He pleases, as being the best thing for you, or to be freed from your trials in the manner He will judge best, without striving to secure rest by individual efforts, which will often prove fruitless. (Battersby, *Meditations*, p. 97)

Reflection

De La Salle's candor to Mr. Gense and Mr. De La Cocherie was surprising because he seldom discussed the many trials that burdened him. Even though his statement to them manifested his suffering, he used his own difficulties to show the two men that God is wise and caring.

At the start of establishing the community, De La Salle's family and friends criticized and abandoned him. Living with and training rough, semiliterate, undisciplined teachers challenged his patience and sense of propriety. All through his career, jealous prelates and hostile rivals undermined and openly attacked his work. Rheumatism crippled him regularly. Jansenists tried to destroy his efforts. And, as he suggested, many of his own Brothers walked out, insulted him, and sided with people who slandered him. At one point, a community even shut its door in his face.

De La Salle persevered because he trusted in God's plan for his good, because he loved the poor children, and because he believed that God called him to his ministry.

✧ Reflect on the sources of your strength. What helps you persevere in times of trouble?

✧ Meditate on De La Salle's conviction that "God will not allow you to be tried beyond your strength."

✧ In his meditation, De La Salle reiterated the biblical teaching that when we are weak and powerless, we become strong because we invite God into our life. Recall a time when you felt powerless or weak, a time when life seemed to be too much and out of your control. Spend time thinking about this situation, who was involved, what happened, how you felt.

Then reflect on how this time of pain and trial has benefited you spiritually, emotionally, or physically. Take the long view of the event. Imagine Jesus with you. In conversation with him, discern how you are a deeper, richer person because of this time of trouble.

✧ Pray a litany to God for the help you need to persevere among present problems; for example, "God of strength, help me be patient with my ailing mother as she loses more of her mental functioning," or "God of strength, help me to bear and to understand Sharon's backbiting."

✧ Today or whenever persevering in your life as a Christian becomes difficult, pray the Jesus Prayer: "Jesus Christ, son of God, have mercy on me."

God's Word

We are subjected to every kind of hardship, but never distressed; we see no way out but we never despair; we are pursued but never cut off; knocked down, but still have some life in us; always we carry with us in our body the death of Jesus so that the life of Jesus, too, may be visible in our body. Indeed, while we are still alive, we are continually being handed over to death, for the sake of Jesus. . . .

But as we have the same spirit of faith as is described in scripture—I believed and therefore I spoke—we, too, believe and therefore we, too, speak, realising that [the one] who raised up the Lord Jesus will raise us up with Jesus in our turn . . . and you as well. You see, everything is for your benefit, so that as grace spreads, so, to the glory of God, thanksgiving may also overflow among more and more people.

That is why we do not waver; indeed, though this outer human nature of ours may be falling into decay, at the same time our inner human nature is renewed day by day. (2 Corinthians 4:8–16)

Closing prayer: "I need only to present myself before you to find solace for my woes. No matter what difficulty I may experience . . . , you are always ready to help me do good. You are my only recourse in my doubts and indecision; you are my refuge when crushing burdens overwhelm me. It is you who inspires and heartens me to do good when I find myself devoid of courage, . . . O God of love." (Adapted from De La Salle, *Method of Mental Prayer*, p. 21)

Meditation 15 ✧

Zeal

Theme: De La Salle understood that strong faith manifests itself in zeal. Rather than remaining dispassionate or halfhearted, De La Salle wanted his Brothers to be filled with zeal for the Good News.

Opening prayer: Fill me now with a passionate attachment to you, my God, and ardent zeal to serve my sisters and brothers.

About De La Salle

With faith, De La Salle made zeal central in the spirituality of the Brothers. He demonstrated his own zeal for his mission throughout his life, but perhaps most dramatically in 1691.

For nearly fifteen years, De La Salle had been working to establish the community. But one obstacle followed another. The community seemed doomed.

> His first concern, in view of the uncertain future, was to make sure that the Institute would possess at least two Brothers capable of maintaining it in case he himself should die. He needed zealous, courageous men, unwaveringly attached to their vocation. Even so, he feared that, discouraged by the difficulties and obstacles they would encounter, disheartened by the contradiction and

opposition they would have to endure, they might lose heart and abandon an enterprise which had as many enemies as there were demons in Hell. . . . Hence he thought it proper to oblige them to this by inspiring them to make, along with him, a vow in the following terms:

"Most Holy Trinity, Father, Son and Holy Spirit, prostrate with the most profound respect before Thy infinite and adorable majesty, we consecrate ourselves entirely to Thee to procure with all our ability and efforts the establishment of the Society of the Christian Schools, in the manner which will seem to us most agreeable to Thee and most advantageous to the said Society.

"And for this purpose, I, John Baptist De La Salle, priest; I, Nicholas Vuyart and I, Gabriel Drolin, from now on and forever until the last surviving one of us, or unto the complete establishment of the said Society, make the vow of association and union to bring about and maintain the said establishment, without being able to withdraw from this obligation, even if only we three remained in the said Society, and if we were obliged to beg for alms and to live on bread alone." (Blain, *De La Salle,* book 2, p. 101)

Pause: Reflect on this question: About what do you have zeal?

De La Salle's Words

What ought to encourage you to have much zeal in your vocation is the fact that you are not only the ministers of God, but also of Jesus Christ and of the church. This is what St. Paul says when he expresses the wish that men should regard those who announce the gospel as ministers of Jesus Christ, whose role is to write the letter dictated by Christ, not with ink but with the Spirit of the living God, not on tablets of stone but on tablets of flesh which are the hearts of children. . . .

Let your zeal give tangible proof that you love those whom God has entrusted to you just as Jesus Christ has loved his church. . . . It is for you to give them this education and training, so that they may become heirs of the kingdom of God and of Jesus Christ our Lord. . . .

Tell the parents . . . what Jesus Christ said about the flock which he shepherds and saves: "I came that they might have life and have it to the full." For this had to be the kind of ardent zeal you had for the salvation of those you teach, when you were led to sacrifice yourself and to spend your whole life to give these children a Christian education and to procure for them the life of grace in this world and eternal life in the next. (*Meditations for the Time of Retreat*, pp. 75–77)

Reflection

"Don't go overboard."
"Be cool."
"Keep an even keel."
"Virtue lies in the middle."

It would be hard to imagine De La Salle making these statements to his Brothers. Great works are not done by lukewarm people. Nothing of significance can be accomplished without zeal, passionate dedication. It seems impossible to think of great writers, artists, or leaders devoid of zeal.

Christian zeal should not be confused with destructive compulsion. Infamous criminals and deranged tyrants are compelled to extreme behavior by destructive forces from within over which they have little control. The zeal that fired De La Salle and that he wanted his Brothers to have manifests itself in constructive creativity, positive energy, and empowerment of other people.

De La Salle radiated zeal and acted dynamically and courageously. Inspired by his faith in the loving God, he zealously acted upon God's call to him.

In *The Power of Myth*, Joseph Campbell remarked: "The influence of a vital person vitalizes, there's no doubt about it. The world without spirit is a wasteland. . . . Any world is a valid world if it's alive. The thing to do is to bring life to it, and the only way to do that is to find in your own case where the life is and become alive yourself" (p. 149). God calls us to be fully alive persons, zealously committed to the Good News and to serving our neighbors.

✧ What sets you ablaze? For what are you zealous? To answer these questions, reflect on times in your life when you felt most alive, energized, when you exuded confidence that what you were about was good and meaningful, when you wished that you could hold the feelings for a lifetime.

✧ Has anything dampened your zeal? Have you lost the focus of your zeal or just put it in a closet for occasional use?

✧ Pray Jesus' promise to you: "I came to bring you the fullness of life."

✧ Bring to mind the faces of those for whom you have a strong, loving commitment. Meditate on ways in which you can nourish your zeal for each one's good.

✧ Jesus came to bring fullness of life and the Reign of God to the hearts and deeds of all people. For fullness of life to come, Christians are called to seek justice for all people, especially people who are poor, sick, powerless, or hungry. How can you zealously bring justice to your family, local community, workplace, and nation? De La Salle's way, teaching poor children, was a humble way of zealously creating a just world. Your ways may be humble too, but also filled with passionate commitment.

✧ De La Salle brought the life of Christ to his world because he was filled with faith and love. These fifteen meditations began with a meditation on faith. Call upon the Holy Spirit to converse with you about how your faith has been strengthened by praying with De La Salle. Ask the Spirit of Wisdom to show you how to be filled with the zeal that comes from faith.

God's Word

How does it help . . . when someone who has never
done a single good act claims to have faith? . . .

. . . It is by my deeds that I will show you my faith.
You believe in the one God—that is creditable enough,
but even the demons have the same belief, and they trem-
ble with fear. Fool! Would you not like to know that faith
without deeds is useless? Was not Abraham our father
justified by his deed, because he offered his son Isaac on
the altar? So you can see that his faith was working together with his deeds; . . . and he received the name
"friend of God."

You see now that it is by deeds, and not only by be-lieving, that someone is justified. . . . As a body without a spirit is dead, so is faith without deeds. (James 2:14–26)

Closing prayer: "My God, I believe and am fully per-suaded that you live and reign in me. Rule over all my interi-or tendencies and exterior movements, so that I may not be master of any of them. Since you, O God, have established your reign within me, it is your right to direct all of these movements. Amen. Alleluia." (Adapted from De La Salle, *Method of Mental Prayer,* p. 34)

FAITH

✧ For Further Reading ✧

De La Salle, John Baptist. *Meditations for the Time of Retreat.* Trans. Augustine Loes. Romeoville, IL: Christian Brothers Conference, 1975.

Salm, Luke. *John Baptist de La Salle: The Formative Years.* Romeoville, IL: Lasallian Publications, 1989.

———. *The Work Is Yours: The Life of Saint John Baptist de La Salle.* Romeoville, IL: Christian Brothers Publications, 1989.

Sauvage, Michel, and Miguel Campos. *St. John Baptist de La Salle: Announcing the Gospel to the Poor.* Trans. Matthew J. O'Connell. Romeoville, IL: Christian Brothers Conference, 1981.

Acknowledgments (*continued*)

The psalms quoted in this book are from *Psalms Anew: In Inclusive Language*, compiled by Nancy Schreck and Maureen Leach (Winona, MN: Saint Mary's Press, 1986). Copyright © 1986 by Saint Mary's Press. Used with permission. All rights reserved.

The scriptural material found on pages 46–47, 52, 59, and 91–92 is freely adapted to make it inclusive regarding gender. These adaptations are not to be understood or used as official translations of the Bible.

All other scriptural quotations used in this book are from the New Jerusalem Bible. Copyright © 1985 by Darton, Longman and Todd, London, and Doubleday, a division of Bantam, Doubleday, Dell Publishing Group, New York. Used with permission.

The excerpts on pages 16, 23, 42–43, 53–54, 55, 66–67, 71–72, 76–77, 93–94, and 98–99 are from *St. John Baptist de La Salle*, by W. J. Battersby, foreword by H. O. Evennett (New York: Macmillan Company, 1957), pages 41 and 71, 290, 52, 230, 134, 126, 65–69, 281, 103–104, and 269, respectively. Copyright © 1958 by W. J. Battersby. Used with permission.

The excerpt on page 17 is from *De La Salle: Letters and Documents*, edited by W. J. Battersby (London: Longmans, Green and Co., 1952), page 257. Used with permission of the publisher.

The excerpts on pages 27–28 and 28 are from *The Work Is Yours: The Life of Saint John Baptist de La Salle*, by Luke Salm (Romeoville, IL: Christian Brothers Publications, 1989), pages 125 and 126, respectively. Copyright © 1989 by Christian Brothers Conference. Used with permission.

The excerpts on pages 28 and 52 are from *A Collection of Various Short Treatises for the Use of the Brothers of the Christian Schools* (New York: La Salle Bureau, 1932), pages 57–59 and 184, respectively.

The excerpts on pages 28, 36–37, 50, and 87–88 are from *The Letters of John Baptist de La Salle*, translation, introduction, and commentary by Bro. Colman Molloy, edited with additional commentary by Bro. Augustine Loes (Romeoville, IL: Lasallian Publications, 1988), respectively on pages 217; 225–226; 248; and 25–27, 36, 142, and 147. Copyright © 1988 by Christian Brothers Conference. Used with permission.

The excerpts on pages 31, 65, and 92 are from *Manual of Piety for the Use of the Brothers of the Christian Schools* (New York: La Salle Bureau, 1935), pages 4, 11, and 72, respectively. Used with permission of La Salle Bureau and La Salle Provincialate.

The excerpt on page 32 is from *De La Salle: Saint and Spiritual Writer*, by W. J. Battersby, foreword by Patrick O'Boyle (London: Longmans, Green and Co., 1950), page 117. Used with permission of the publisher.

The excerpts on pages 33, 54–55, 83–84, 89, and 103–104 are from *Meditations for the Time of Retreat*, by John Baptist de La Salle, translated by Bro. Augustine Loes, introduction by Bro. Miguel Campos (Romeoville, IL: Christian Brothers Conference, 1975), pages 57–58, 56, 47, 54 and 80, and 75–77, respectively. Copyright © 1975 by Christian Brothers Conference. Used with permission.

The excerpts on pages 37, 61–62, 67, 72–73, 78, 94–95, and 99 are from *De La Salle: Meditations*, edited by W. J. Battersby (London: Waldegrave Publishers, 1964), pages 284, 309, 174, 40, 546–547, 148 and 400, and 97, respectively. Copyright © 1964 by Waldegrave Publishers. Used with permission.

The excerpts on pages 37, 38, 39, 41, 55–56, 101, and 107 are from *Explanation of the Method of Mental Prayer*, by John Baptist de La Salle, translated by Richard Arnandez (Romeoville, IL: Christian Brothers Conference, n.d.), pages 4, 8, 24–25, 32, 63, 21, and 34, respectively. Used with permission of Christian Brothers Conference.

The excerpts on pages 43–44, 49–50, and 74 are from *The Life of John Baptist de La Salle, Founder of the Brothers of the Christian Schools*, book 1, by Canon John Baptist Blain, translated by Bro. Richard Arnandez (Romeoville, IL: Christian Brothers Conference, n.d.), pages 123, 61, and 124, respectively. Used with permission of Christian Brothers Conference.

The excerpt on pages 48–49 is from *The Life of John Baptist de La Salle, Founder of the Brothers of the Christian Schools*, book 3, by Canon John Baptist Blain, translated by Bro. Richard Arnandez (Romeoville, IL: Christian Brothers Conference, n.d.), pages 40–41. Used with permission of Christian Brothers Conference.

The excerpt on pages 60–61 is from *The Conduct of the Schools of Jean-Baptiste de La Salle*, translation and introduction by F. de La Fontainerie (New York: McGraw-Hill Book Company, 1935), page 55. Copyright © 1935 by McGraw-Hill Book Company. Used with permission.

The excerpts on pages 83 and 102–103 are from *The Life of John Baptist de La Salle, Founder of the Brothers of the Christian Schools*, book 2, by Canon John Baptist Blain, translated by Bro. Richard Arnandez, FSC (Romeoville, IL: Christian Brothers Conference, n.d.), pages 95–96 and 101, respectively. Used with permission of Christian Brothers Conference.

The excerpt on pages 104–105 is from *The Power of Myth*, by Joseph Campbell, with Bill Moyers, edited by Betty Sue Flowers (New York: Doubleday, 1988), page 149. Copyright © 1988 by Apostrophe S Productions and Alfred van der Marck Editions.

Titles in the Companions for the Journey series:

Praying with Julian of Norwich
Praying with Francis of Assisi
Praying with Catherine of Siena
Praying with John Baptist de La Salle
Praying with Teresa of Ávila   Available fall 1990

Order from

Saint Mary's Press
Terrace Heights
Winona, MN 55987-0560